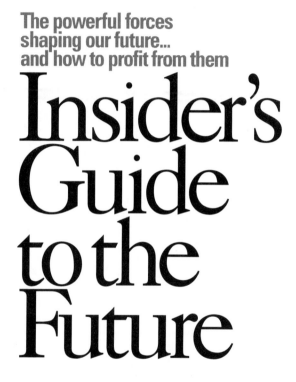

The powerful forces
shaping our future...
and how to profit from them

Insider's Guide to the Future

BY EDITH WEINER & ARNOLD BROWN
WEINER, EDRICH, BROWN, INC.

Boardroom® publishes the advice of expert authorities
in many fields.
The use of a book is not a substitute for legal, accounting or
other professional services. Consult a competent professional
for answers to your specific questions.

Library of Congress Cataloging in Publication Data
Main entry under title:

Insider's Guide to the Future

   1. Life skills—United States.   I. Bottom line personal.
ISBN 0-88723-148-9

Printed in the United States of America

11497

TABLE OF CONTENTS

INTRODUCTION

Now we all know the terror Columbus' sailors felt in 1492. Every day they found themselves sailing farther away from the known and deeper into the unknown. So it is with us. Like those sailors, we have left behind a time in which each day is like its predecessor and in which the landmarks never change (or change so slowly that the differences are almost imperceptible).

We have embarked on a journey where every day we see a new horizon, and the world (however flawed) that we were comfortable with is fast fading.

A major difference between us and those sailors of 500 years ago is that we have much more information than they had. We have the charts and maps they lacked. But, somehow, the future seems just as unseeable and frightening to us as it did to them.

We have to know more than the distance between here and there. Having that information was not enough then, and it is not enough now. We still have to be able to interpret it, to translate it from the abstract to the practical. We have to know...

- which course to take
- what we can expect to see when we get there
- what parts of our destination will be viable
- what tools we will need to survive there.

With all that Columbus thought he knew, he still wound up in a place that surprised him, in a world that changed the course of all to come.

For 35 years after the end of World War II, the period we now call the Post-Industrial Era, we had a rare combination of high economic growth and low personal risk. It was not necessary to choose between growth and security. But—no more. That time is gone, propelled off the stage by the arrival of cheap and abundant information and greater competition (created by the information revolution).

The ocean we are now crossing is one of rapid and massive social and economic changes, driven by technological revolutions that are unprecedented in human history. It is a period of profound and wrenching transformation.

One of the things resulting from this transformation—
something that has happened every time humans have under-
gone great change—is an abundance of Gloomy Gusses.
We now have a large group of "endists." They pontificate
about the end of history...and the end of science...and the
end of compassion...or whatever. Their problem is that they
see only half of what's happening—they see the ends but not
the beginnings. They see the glass half empty, when it's really half full—and filling fast.

It is our intention in this book to help illuminate for
you the beginnings...

CHAPTER 1

THE COMING ECONOMY

This latest leg of the journey we are taking into the future has been given many names: "The Knowledge Economy," "The Information Society," "The Service Economy," "The Leisure Society," "The Communications Economy." But these terms describe only parts of the unfolding world, not the whole. Now a vision of the whole is in our sights, and we can give it a better name.

But first, we need to back up a bit. It should be understood that each new economy or society is not a replacement. Rather, it is layered over what came before. No economy disappears. Instead, through efficiency, it uses a shrinking proportion of the workforce. The United States is still an agricultural economy, but it is no longer an agricultural society. Less than three percent of our workforce is now tied to the farm.

Similarly, we are still an industrial economy, even though the industrial workforce has declined sharply to less than 20% of workers. Just as the industrial economy was layered onto the agricultural, the post-industrial economy was layered onto them. And now, another layer is being rapidly added.

There are three major factors—driving forces—that create this layering effect...

ADVANCING EFFICIENCIES IN TECHNOLOGY

Machines such as the cotton gin and the mechanical reaper radically reduced the need for human labor in agriculture. As machines become cheaper than people, technological displacement occurs, further accelerating the reduction in employment. Then, these new technological advances spur new consumer products, and buyers expect higher technological capabilities from sellers.

In the 200 years or so since the Industrial Revolution began, technology has eliminated many jobs. But it has created far more jobs than it has destroyed. And the tendency for the new jobs is to be better and higher paying. All this is what economist Joseph Schumpeter called "creative destruction"—dismantling the old so that the new can flourish. As proof of Schumpeter's thesis, during the last 200 years, Gross Domestic Product (GDP) per capita in the developed world has grown at an average of 1.6% per year, resulting in the doubling of income per head every 44 years. Prior to that, GDP growth averaged less than two tenths of one percent a year, and income took 500 years to double.

DISENCHANTMENT WITH THE PSYCHOLOGICAL REWARDS AND PHYSICAL STRESS OF THE EXISTING ORDER

The hard labor and long hours of agriculture, and the uncertainty of reward, made it easier for displaced farm workers to accept a shift to employment in manufacturing. Similarly, the low status associated with industrial labor, along with the hard work, encouraged people to acquire more education and move to white collar work. But work/family conflict, commuting, competition for jobs and employment instability have taken much of the appeal out of office work. People now move closer to work in the suburbs, where offices are relocating, and they do more telecommuting (working from remote locations with portable and desktop computers, faxes, etc.). In the marketplace, the slowness of transportation and communication under the old system becomes unacceptable, and consumers flock to retailers and suppliers who deliver goods and services faster and more conveniently.

HEIGHTENED COMPETITION IN THE MARKETPLACE

Competition forces businesses to become more efficient. Traditionally, in Western cultures, the easiest way to reduce overhead is by cutting labor costs. So now, even in post-industrial businesses, we have seen worldwide announcements of layoffs. Companies have seen reductions in the tens of thousands of employees. Furthermore, competitive pressures create new entries into the economy, and this entrepreneurial fervor woos customers away from existing products and existing distribution channels.

Together, these three factors act powerfully to cut employment in the dominant sector of an economy and to shift marketplace behavior. People find work in new sectors of the economy, further spurring the growth of these. Over time, new community and work patterns emerge, eventually leading to a new society.

In the past, these changes took place gradually over a period of many years. (In fact, many countries are still mainly agricultural societies.) What we are seeing now, particularly in advanced countries, is that the process has been very much speeded up. Indeed, the current transformation is taking place in less time than it takes for an adult to complete his or her working life. This is the new element. This is what has discombobulated countries at the leading edge —not the change, but the pace of change.

One important consequence of this rapidity of change is the uncertainty it creates. This uncertainty is felt most by employees who are more than halfway through their work life. And this is the first time new or recent college graduates believe that their education won't serve them for more than just a few decades. This is particularly true in technological fields—it has been estimated that an electronic engineer's knowledge is outdated five years after graduation—but it applies more and more to other disciplines as well.

We now live in an age where we find our food relatively inexpensive, and our industrial commodities, except for automobiles, in cheap and abundant supply: Hair dryers for $7, watches for $1.98, and even refrigerators, TVs, washing machines and air conditioners affordable for most Americans. And we see the price of post-industrial goods plummeting—a computer-chip-based musical birthday card costs $3 and holds the processing capacity of what once took up an entire room of computer equipment. A long-distance call can cost a few pennies. A pocket calculator can be had for $3. People have begun, therefore, to turn their attention to those things that enhance their senses of self-worth, mental agility, physical health and spiritual happiness.

We addressed three questions to come up with a name and model for the newly arriving economy…

- *Where will people find work?*
- *Where will people spend their disposable income?*
- *What will be the "M.O."…the modus operandi?*

To describe the new pattern, we needed a word that reflected the highly personalized focus of a fast-moving world. So we coined the term **Emotile**. It is a combination word, putting together what seem to be the two most salient aspects of the coming new world:

Emotion—the focus on heightened concern for personal well-being, and

Motility—the impermanent, fast-moving, short-lived mobility of all relationships and ways of organizing.

The charts that follow show the layering of economies and the **Emotile Era** in diagram form.

The five major categories to the left of the second chart depict *job expansion, business growth* and *increased expenditures of disposable income.*

On the right are the three *major areas in which ways of doing things will radically change.* Applying a knowledge of any or all of these eight factors will guide organizations and individuals through the rough waters they are currently experiencing, and propel them more profitably and comfortably into the wondrous world unfolding ahead.

The chapters that follow will explore each of these eight factors in more detail.

U.S. EXPERIENCE
LAYERING OF ECONOMIES/
REFORMATION OF SOCIETIES

THE AGRICULTURAL ECONOMY
—Led to—THE AGRICULTURAL SOCIETY

This dominated until the first global applications of industrialization (18th century).

THE INDUSTRIAL ECONOMY
—Led to—THE INDUSTRIAL SOCIETY

This lasted for about 170 years, from c. 1800 to 1970.

THE POST-INDUSTRIAL ECONOMY
—Led to—THE POST-INDUSTRIAL SOCIETY

Began about 1950 and rose to dominance in the 1960s through 2005.

THE EMOTILE ECONOMY
—is leading to—THE EMOTILE SOCIETY

Began in earnest about 1992 and rises to dominance about 2005.

THE EMOTILE ECONOMY/SOCIETY

EMOTIONAL
Heightened concern for personal well-being

Where Money Will Flow and Jobs Will Be Created

Augmentation of Intellect	Health	Security	Personal Services	Spiritual Fulfillment
Education Information Entertainment	Physical & Mental	Financial Security	Customized	Religious & Ethnic
		Personal Safety	Macro and Micro	Leisure Travel Self-Discovery
				Stewardship Public and Community Enterprise

MOTILE
Fast-moving, portable, non-fixed

Ways of Organizing and Affiliating

Ways of getting things done	*Ways of building relationships*	*Ways of viewing the world*
Manufacturing	Family & Household	Transcendental
Working	Friends & Community	Relativistic
Communicating	Occupational	
Delivering Goods & Services		

CHAPTER 2

AUGMENTATION

OF INTELLECT

The first major growth area has three components: Information, education and entertainment. In the Post-Industrial Era, these were three separate and fast-growing industries. Tomorrow, the businesses that pursue each of these will also have to be involved in the other two. And it will be difficult to be in any business without being in at least two of the three.

As a sign of what will be, Intel, the major producer of chips, is now also investing more money in start-up businesses that are entertainment- or consumer-oriented, such as Cnet—a San Francisco company that develops shows for the Internet and Cable TV. Intel hopes to ensure a horizontal market for its products. So does Microsoft, with its spectacular entrances into entertainment and news. Bill Gates and Andrew Grove are pioneers in what will be the merger of information, education and entertainment. So is George Lucas, whose special effects in *Star Wars* will lead to a host of new applications in industrial, military, home, Hollywood, TV and educational environments.

Some have already appeared. For example, special effects created for Hollywood were adopted by Ford Motor Company for the liquid molding of auto parts. The U.S. Army's Land Warrior weapon is a conventional M16 rifle fitted with a thermal camera, an infrared laser rangefinder and a digital compass, all linked to software, from topographic maps to images of buildings, and all able to be transmitted to other members of the platoon. This was not a high-cost outcome of military R&D, but rather an agglomeration of commercial off-the-shelf components that were part of the new infrastructure called the Information Superhighway.

What is the Information Superhighway anyway? It is a more or less loosely networked system of roads carrying information, education and entertainment onto major avenues that merge into the Broadway of the future, with the U.S. leading the way. The merging of publishing, computing, telecommunications, schooling, newscasting, movie-making, gaming, televising, medical diagnosing, industrial prototyping, database warehousing and many more mega-industries of yesterday into a conglomerate-based multi-media super-structure of tomorrow is now beginning to take shape on that Broadway at an incredibly rapid pace.

Regulation and legislation plod behind all this because there are few precedents and fewer clear standards of shoulds and shouldn'ts. Copyright, intellectual property, royalties, license fees, patent protection—in a world where much of this has already been exposed to uncertainties, the issues will become more complex and difficult. Our accounting systems are befuddled by the need to measure non-financials, such as intellectual assets, which elude quantitative analysis.

Knowledge is becoming *the* resource rather than a resource. In 1994, Skandia, the Swiss insurance giant, hired Leif Edvinsson to become the world's first director of intellectual capital. He approached this position from the belief that intellectual assets exceed by many times the value of assets that appear on balance sheets, and they can be reused over and over again to create more value.

What will intellectual assets become, now that we can distinguish between various types of intelligence? Brain scans linked to 3-D virtual reality systems will increasingly show us the different forms of intelligence, the characteristics of problem-solving, the male-female distinctions in the brain, the sleeping and waking states of learning and memory, and even the ways music can enhance brain function...

At the Beckman Institute for Advanced Science and Technology (University of Illinois), researchers, including electrical engineers, psychologists, biophysicists, computer scientists, molecular biologists, linguists, chemists, and physicists, are already studying three major areas: Biological Intelligence (the ways in which neurally based systems display intelligent behavior and how that could be used in the design of intelligent devices), Molecular and Electronic Nanostructures, and Human Computer Intelligent Interaction.

More and more books, newspapers and magazines will come on line, creating interactive forums, role-playing and an explosion of intellectual fireworks. We'll see many more "zines"—small-circulation periodicals, published by individuals with computers and peripherals that cost a tiny fraction of what it used to take to start a magazine a decade ago.

In this process of focusing on intellectual growth, new industries, large and tiny, conglomerate and niche, are emerging to capitalize on the rush to augment mind, creativity, imagination and improvement of the body by way of the brain.

ON THE EDGE OF INFORMATION

Fuzzy logic, developed conceptually in the 1960s by Latfi Zadeh, an Iraqi-American scientist, enables software to have the "multivalued" and "continuous" reasoning of the human mind, as apart from discrete yes/no and mutually exclusive sets. For example, it enables a system to "think" what three seemingly disconnected things may have in common, such as jewelry, hair implants and cologne—all used as adornments to make one more attractive. The ability to think in gradations and connections will lead to new businesses and industries that enhance current products and services, in everything from kitchen appliances to the content of our pocketbooks.

We are moving toward "embedded systems," the technology that will transfer the Internet into a mass-market presence everywhere—and in everything—the car, TV, phone, meters, etc. Embedded systems are tiny, fortified computers of the sort already embedded in industrial and consumer products, from antilock brakes to VCRs to microwaves. Today, 90% of the world's microprocessors are not in PCs but in these common household or electronics products, and they are becoming Internet-ready. This automated but miniaturized, embedded and dedicated Net connectivity would offer 1/100 the memory of a large-scale PC operating system, at about 1/10th the cost. The factory floor, the home security system, the patient-doctor relationship, the processes by which we meter, assess, manage and deliver—all would be capable of remote interconnectivity and all will be transformed by this information revolution.

Most government data are based upon the division of the economy into two sectors—those businesses that produce goods and those that provide services. But with so much of what is to come derived from information, it is important to gear up for new measurements and statistical accounting. For example, the service sector seems to be creating more of the job gains, while the information sector is posting the productivity gains. That may not be the case when we begin to couple information technology with two service areas that are expanding exponentially—education and entertainment.

EDUCATION

Earlier in U.S. history, education and schooling were separate. Only the wealthy and intellectually dedicated had much schooling. For the rest, much of their education was gotten through "street smarts," local news, the church and on-the-job apprenticing.

In the Agricultural Era, there was the one-room schoolhouse for students of all ages, which most children left when they reached their teen years and went to work full-time. With the introduction of the Industrial Era came the need to keep children out of the newly competitive, urban workforce, so attendance and age mandates were initiated. Neighborhood schools were set up along age cohort lines, with a strengthened thrust toward public education. Those who were not likely to pursue higher education got a grounding in commercial or vocational skills.

But with the Post-Industrial Era came America's Sputnik-initiated push toward widescale math and science literacy, extending education down below kindergarten and up through graduate school. Credentialism reigned. Without the proper academic credentials, good jobs that previously required only a high school diploma were no longer to be easily had.

Now we move into the **Emotile Era**, into a time when education increasingly is perceived to be lifelong. It will begin in the womb, where many mothers already stimulate embryos by playing music and eating foods guaranteed to bolster intelligence. Preschools, often starting shortly after birth, will stimulate and prepare the children of "haves" for elementary school. There will be a big and growing market in software for two- and three-year-olds. Post-graduate degrees at the other end of academic life will be increasingly attractive to those in their 30s, 50s and even 70s. Adult education will continue to expand, with training for "re-skilling" and "the learning organization" being just two of the many growing businesses in this arena.

As public lower schools are seen as inadequate in this new environment, private schooling will boom. Already, more than one in 10 U.S. children attend private or parochial schools. Around Boston, independent private schools are enrolling about seven percent more children every year. In some states, like Oregon and Washington, there are waiting lists of over three years.

As we shift from a Post-Industrial to an **Emotile Era**, there will be questions about what and how to teach children. For example, several billion dollars have been spent on several million computers for classrooms, but does this actually contribute to declining literacy, as videos take over from the written word? Will computers dampen intellectual debate, reason and logic in favor of shallow bursts of information?

Education will no longer be about schooling alone. Video games and interactive programs and systems are now delivering everything from biology lessons to geography lessons to young and old alike, anywhere, anytime. By the year 2000, parents will be spending more than $1 billion a year on software for at-home learning, and much of this will be in the form of "edutainment"— an attractive mix of fun and learning, which wrests control from the teacher and puts it in the hands of the student.

About half a million American children were being home-schooled in 1990, increasing about 15% a year, and the trend will be sped up by digital technology, such as the Internet and educational software.

At the higher educational levels there will be more "Virtual Universities," such as BioMOO (Biology Multiple-User dimension, Object-Orient) run out of the Bioinformatics Unit of the Weizman Institute of Science in Jerusalem. It is a computer program/facility that "houses" more than 300 biologists from three continents and dozens of fields who collaborate in cyberspace. There is a BioMOO lounge, where a MOO tutorial is given. Virtual doors lead to laboratories, a library, a cafe, seminar rooms, etc.

Psychologists and educators will increasingly explore video games that attract girls to computing systems as much as their male counterparts, to enable them to find this new learning tool less daunting and more friendly. This is developing in the adult world, too, where major strides are being made to encourage women to use computers as much as men.

As software developers engage two-year-olds and make them computer literate before they are literate, pushing education *down* in years, single parents and working mothers will seek to push education *out*, by expanding before- and after-school programs and summer activities.

And employers will continue pushing education *up*. Everywhere they are demanding higher incoming credentials and career resilience through retraining, re-education, continued education and constant learning. More of those employees who would once have made do with high school diplomas (and vocational training) will now seek out community colleges. In 1994, about six million students were enrolled for credit in community colleges, a 250% increase since the late 1960s.

Up to now there was little incentive for Japanese students to take post-graduate courses. France has three times as many undergraduate students continuing on into post-graduate work as Japan, and the U.S. has eight times as many. But Japan's new graduate schools indicate the new seriousness there in pushing up education beyond undergraduate studies.

As we move toward the 21st century, higher education will become more entrepreneurial, and more will be offered through the open market. More students of all ages will be educated based on their own adaptive ability to grasp the material, as opposed to "age appropriate" groupings. Innovations in computer-adaptive testing (CAT), for example, will force new ways to administer and evaluate standard tests. Testing at one's convenience, at testing centers where identity is confirmed, will likely one day replace standardized test times and dates. And just about all education, at every age level, will include entertaining and state-of-the-art graphics and interactive dialogue.

The **Emotile Era** will usher in the age of edutainment for the entire population, old and young and, yes, even rich and poor. The marketplace for goods and services in education will expand greatly. But we will still be scratching our heads and wondering—are we teaching the right things, and are we teaching them right? No knowledge of what's to come will ever satisfactorily put those questions to rest.

ENTERTAINMENT

It's not just education that will rest heavily on entertainment. So will almost every other endeavor. Keen competition for the customer's time, money and attention could mean that "boring" retailing will be the path to oblivion. People used to buy "sneakers" for $3, and now we spend from $55 to $150 for "athletic shoes." What is being bought here? A great deal of information technology in the design of the materials and the production of the shoes, education as to which shoes perform best under what circumstances, and the massive amount of entertainment that goes into the branding and marketing of that shoe.

Entertainment will underpin a great deal of the coming era. The entertainment and recreation industries are already adding upwards of 200,000 workers each year, or 12% of all net new employment. And, as we stated earlier, it is the entertainment industry that is increasingly the driving force behind new technology development, not the military, as was once the case.

Theater, once projected to be in its death throes, is now booming. Live concerts are a multibillion dollar business. Computers will revolutionize entertainment even further. There are now interactive recorded music CDs and CD-ROMs on the market, and major record companies will be meshing the picture and sound of music videos with the interactive capacity of the personal computer.

More travelers in the U.S. will couple vacationing with educational experiences, with younger Americans being even more interested in this than their parents. Almost half of U.S. adults now planning a trip say they already intend to visit a historic site on vacation, and two in five plan to visit a cultural site.

AND SO...

Around the world we see the integration of information, entertainment and education capturing more time, interest and disposable income. And in the **Emotile Era**, cultures will mesh, telecommunications will enhance interactivity, and the global thrust of this trend will escalate.

How it has begun...

The governor of Daqahliya, Egypt, blamed satellite dishes that bring in Western programming for increased violence and school absenteeism. In the same country, the governor of Damietta blamed his people's deteriorating furniture industry on workers stuck in front of sex scenes shown on the satellite dish.

Iranian viewers, bored with state-run TV programs, are in large numbers tuning in to Rupert Murdoch's STAR TV. The mullahs are aware that people are demanding liberty to be informed, educated and entertained in new ways in their own homes.

The Internet is affording Asians the opportunity for free expression, from soft porn to hard political debate.

While governments try to clamp down on the press, citizens are attracted to computer networks to criticize, inform, educate and entertain.

Asia has more than 100,000 computers connected to the Internet, and China plans to connect as many as a quarter of a million computers.

Outside Beijing, the Bilingual Educational Computer Company develops animated, interactive CD-ROM programs to teach English and sells these worldwide. There are software designers in India at the cutting edge of 3D imaging technology for diagnosing brain disorders. Malaysia and Singapore have placed great emphasis on math and science training for the future.

And how it will go...

Digital HDTV (high definition TV), promoted as the ultimate in home technology, will deliver all manner of digital services into homes and offices across America and, eventually, the world.

This future of choice, interactivity, access and on-demand will permeate almost all corners of the globe. There are already 700 million people in the world who earn over $10,000 per year, the point at which a customer will shop the world for entertainment, information and education as well as all other consumables.

While the U.S. is clearly currently ahead of the rest of the world in the development and deployment of information technology, and may remain so for the foreseeable future, this **Emotile Era** is embracing the youth of the globe everywhere. The digital revolution is driven by the young. They will no longer accept boredom, and they will not accept boundaries, which in virtual reality and cyberspace do not have much relevance. While video game formats introduce them and their elders to quantum mechanics, organic chemistry and geometry, the world is open to them as they increasingly populate and shape the **Emotile Era**.

CHAPTER 3

HEALTH

PHYSICAL HEALTH

People, particularly Americans, will be increasingly concerned—one could even say obsessed—with not only health, but wellness. Wellness is more than just absence of disease—it means feeling good about one's physical and mental condition.

To some extent, this focus will be a natural result of the aging of the population in all industrial countries. But it will also be very much a consequence of the intense focus on self that has characterized the American Baby Boom, that one-third of the population that has set the agenda for the U.S. since the 1960s. As Boomers age, as they experience the customary health concerns that accompany aging, they will increasingly feel an anxious entitlement to wellness. So you can expect continued growth of the U.S. healthcare industry, an increasing percentage of GDP allocated to healthcare, and an explosion of jobs in this sector.

But that's only part of the story. The fact is, spending on wellness will add up to considerably more than the official statistics. It will rightfully include spending on athletic equipment and clothing, diet programs, "cosmeceuticals" (cosmetics that promise or imply some health or wellness benefit), bottled water, aromatherapy, stress reduction, self-help and victimization books and programs...and so on. All these will increasingly be driven here and around the world by a desire for physical and mental well-being and a belief in one's entitlement to that ideal.

And, as in other parts of the economy, we will see a massive entrepreneurial revolution in the healthcare field. For example, revenues of companies that treat patients at home rather than in hospitals have already grown from $1.3 billion to $8.5 billion in 10 years.

TECHNOLOGY

While cloning has gotten much attention, the greatest technological engine of change in health will be genetic engineering. Within a very few years, as part of a massive global effort, scientists will have mapped the entire human genetic structure—the *genome*. All the 50,000 to 100,000 human genes, comprised of some three billion bits of information, will be known. And then we will be on the road to complete understanding and control of the ability to alter individual humans' health.

The possibilities include correcting genetic defects, improving the immune system, creating genetically altered foods and drugs that treat or correct specific disorders and diseases, making people smarter and making them live longer and healthier. Conditions such as Alzheimer's, breast cancer, high cholesterol, multiple sclerosis, osteoporosis, Down's syndrome, and just about all the other innate afflictions that have bedeviled humanity since time began will come to be susceptible to treatment, prevention and even elimination.

Another major driver of change will be information technology. Healthcare in the future will be based on smart cards, microprobes and instantaneously shared information. Coming...telecommunications that will link sources of information about illnesses and treatments, new diagnostic and treatment techniques, providers, and patients into one interconnected network. Each person will have available at all times an individualized medical expert system that will diagnose, prescribe and even make available remotely based treatment.

People living far away from the best hospitals will still be able to get the best treatment, using robotics and image-guided electronics.

Already, CompuServe subscribers can ask a medical bulletin board, MedSOS, questions about their health and get answers from doctors. There are a multitude of CD-ROMs on health, including some that advise people on where to find the best hospitals and managed-care companies. Home medical testing kits will become increasingly available, less expensive and easier to use.

AGING

Populations will continue to age, particularly in the developed world, but also in the developing world. Recent predictions are that America's population of people 85 and older is expected to increase by six times by 2050.

In Japan, one-fifth of the population is now 80 or older and, by 2050, it will be one-third. Ever since 1950, the number of people over 100 in the developed countries has doubled every decade. In some countries, the annual rate of increase is over 10%.

What is significant is that what we have always believed about aging will not necessarily be true tomorrow. It was believed that aging always meant infirmity and disability. Yet studies now tell us that, for at least the last couple of decades, levels of chronic disability among older Americans actually declined—and this decline was more pronounced among those over 85! Similar results have been found in Sweden, Norway, Japan and the United Kingdom. Not surprisingly, these changes correlate with education levels and financial well-being. We can anticipate that education levels will continue to increase and that older people will continue to enjoy financial security, so it is reasonable to expect that disability and dependency rates will continue to go down among older people.

It has always been believed that the human brain declines with age. It was accepted wisdom that, as we get older, our brain cells die and are not replaced. Over time, this would lead to a significant drop in some mental capacities, particularly memory. But new research shows us that these declines are not inevitable, they do not happen at the same rate to all people, and to some extent, when they do happen, they can be reversed.

We are also discovering that aging is not necessarily inevitable. Through genetic manipulation, skin treatments and lifestyle changes (diet, exercise, etc.), we will keep more people younger longer than we had ever imagined. The fountain of youth may indeed be within our reach.

FOOD

The American people more and more will see food as being something more than food...it will also be a means to health. Demand for food products that are low in calories and fat is already growing at a rate of over five percent a year. Artificial sweetener sales are expected to be close to $1 billion a year in the U.S. by the year 2000.

Intake of fruit and vegetables has increased significantly over the last 20 years. And the increase is expected to accelerate as the Baby Boomers enter middle age in large numbers. From 1975 to 1995, annual consumption of red meat per person in the U.S. went from 142 pounds to 123 pounds, and the consumption of poultry went from 49 pounds to 90 pounds. As the industrial world eats healthier, the developing world grows more of a propensity for meat. However, with the increasingly rapid and global spread of information and food substitution technologies, we may see global eating habits becoming healthier overall.

MENTAL HEALTH

The distinction between mind and body is increasingly seen as an artificial distinction. New information, coming in almost daily now, will continue to tell us over and over again that mind and body are inextricably and thoroughly linked. These examples cover the spectrum:

- Dr. William Fry of Stanford University reports that laughter can increase white blood cell activity, a key factor in fighting off bacteria, and can even improve muscle tone. Humor and comedy will be increasingly valued for health reasons.
- Numerous studies have demonstrated that different moods are directly related to levels of immune system activity. Stress actually weakens the immune system, and this in turn can affect susceptibility to cancer. Stress management will be a major field of study and marketplace activity.

- An increasing number of medical authorities now believe that prayer can improve health. The eminent cardiologist, Dr. Randolph Byrd, conducted a study showing that coronary care patients who received daily prayers had fewer complications and life-threatening events than those who didn't—less congestive heart failure, fewer cardiopulmonary arrests and less pneumonia. You can expect religion and spirituality to play a larger role in the healthcare system.

- HMOs, such as New England's Harvard-Pilgrim Health Care Plan, have authorized participating physicians to use relaxation techniques and other forms of alternative medicine in treating patients. These forms of treatment will grow in market share.

- A study by Dr. David Spiegel of Stanford showed women who have breast cancer die at a higher rate if their husbands cope poorly with the stress. Disease management will increasingly come to include psychological and family counseling.

- Half of all medical schools now offer some form of mind-body instruction, such as relaxation and massage. New specialties will arise that combine Eastern and Western practices.

- Men who say they feel hopeless die at higher rates from heart disease, cancer and other causes, reported the California Department of Health Services.

That last point is particularly significant. A recent study from the National Institute of Mental Health reports that 45 million Americans—about 28% of the population—suffer from mental disorders, addictions or dependency. Countless millions more express feelings of victimization, a sense of being powerless. And this, of course, is exacerbated by the many and massive changes now going on in our economy and our society. The more oppressed people feel, the more they will feel that they are helpless victims of forces beyond their control, and the more their physical health is likely to be adversely affected.

And, consequently, the more opportunities there will be to provide products and services—inside and outside the healthcare establishment—that will help people cope.

We believe that there will be no upper limit on health-care spending. The American people, as we pointed out earlier, will be obsessed with a personal sense of well-being. Society will no longer base its perceptions of wellness on the *disease* model—instead, it will be the *dis-ease* model. Whatever undermines one's sense of well-being—whether it's a disease or a chronic impairment or hair loss or a flat chest or a personality problem—people will believe it should be treatable and will be willing to pay for treatment. And this area will see a great increase in employment opportunities, as the healthcare focus swells to mammoth proportions.

CHAPTER 4

SECURITY

FINANCIAL SECURITY

There will be an ever more overwhelming concern in the middle class—particularly the managerial and professional elements—for personal financial safety. Our general culture has been built on optimism and fair play. If you played by the rules, if you got an education, prepared yourself for a career, applied yourself to the interests of your employer—if you did all these things, you could be assured of continued and growing prosperity for yourself—and for your children.

Recent events are changing that belief system—and will continue to do so as we move into the next century. The feeling will be that even if you do play by the rules, you may still lose the game. Many will feel that rather than being able to control their destinies by their actions, their destinies will play out regardless of what they do...that they may excel at their jobs and still become victims of downsizing or reengineering or outdated skills. The word "victim" is key here.

A recent Roper Starch survey reported that Americans are increasingly worried about both current and long-range financial issues. Almost half of the people now worry about having enough money to live on when they retire. Forty-nine percent are afraid of being overwhelmed by medical bills in the event of a serious or prolonged illness.

More than 30% question whether they will be able to pay for major household repairs. And nearly 40% worry about how long they will be able to pay the rent or the mortgage. In particular, many Baby Boomers fear that the Social Security system will go broke just when they would need it most.

Doubts and fears such as these are creating a situation in which many in the middle class see powerful forces for change as personal attacks on them—on what they are and what they believe. They will feel victimized for some time to come. They will tend more and more to want to return to a past, mythical or otherwise, in which the game was still played according to the rules. So they will turn in larger numbers to religion or Elvis or the Brady Bunch —a romanticized vision of a past that is remembered as easier, simpler and much more comfortable.

They will also fervently search for financial security. Concerned about losing their jobs or being forced into early retirement, faced with the possible absence or decline of pension income (including Social Security) and loss of health insurance, they will be further disheartened by the continuation of such trends as the decline of employment in the *Fortune* 500 industrial companies. These companies employed 16.3 million people in 1979 compared with well under 12 million today.

In addition, many more people will find themselves part of what has been called the "sandwich generation"— they will have responsibility (financial and otherwise) for both their children and their parents.

This will result in an increasing emphasis on self-reliance, expressed in careers as professionals and entrepreneurs rather than as employees. And this will put most, if not all, of the burden on each individual to prepare himself/herself to be in some way employable.

Out of all this will come a perception that people are on their own. For many, the corporate womb will no longer exist. And even where it does still exist, it will be less a womb than a waiting room. Employees of corporations increasingly will be told that the responsibility for their future financial well-being is theirs, not their employer's. Most pension plans, for example, have already shifted from "defined benefit" (guaranteeing a specific future income) to "defined contribution" (with no future income amount guaranteed). And, in many cases, the shift has been to

35

401(k) plans—now covering more than 40 million Americans—which make employees fully responsible for investing the money.

The gloomy sense of the future, as usual, is probably overstated. A closer look tells us that some remarkable things have been happening, and are likely to continue to happen, in the financial sphere.

In 1980, bank deposits in the U.S. were 11 times larger than mutual funds. Today, mutual fund assets exceed $3 trillion and are larger than the combined deposits of the 100 largest U.S. banks.

There are now more stocks owned by 401(k) plans than by all of the traditional pension funds. Fidelity Investments, which handles investments for a substantial number of 401(k)s, alone accounts for almost 10% of the daily trading volume on the New York Stock Exchange.

Recent studies show that more people in their 30s and 40s are saving earlier than their parents did. Not able to count on pensions or Social Security, these younger workers are swelling the coffers of financial institutions. A survey for the Employee Benefit Research Institute (EBRI) found that more than 60% of today's workers are saving for retirement, and they started at an average age of 30! By contrast, among today's retirees, only 55% saved for retirement, and they started saving at an average age of 38.

The leading edge of the Baby Boom reached 50 in 1996. This means that the bulk of this massive age group is entering their peak earning years, and this means in turn that we should see an incredible surge of savings. A study by McKinsey projects that net household financial assets in the developed world will balloon by nearly $12 trillion by 2005. Most of this great increase in available capital will not sit passively in low-paying bank deposits, as happened in the past. It will be assertive capital, striving for high returns and fueling a global economic expansion of unprecedented proportions.

Another significant development will be the continuing explosion in female entrepreneurship. Women-owned businesses in the U.S. now number eight million. One-third of all businesses in the U.S. are already women-owned. But women will expand the financial security market for other reasons as well—their insecurity as they age will be amplified by more singlehood and divorce, fewer or no children, longer life spans and a continued lack of training in financial self-management. As they, too, face the diminished promise of pensions and government support, they will create an important shift in the marketplace. While Macy's looked to Bloomingdale's as its competitor, its real competition for the female customer's disposable income will be coming from mutual funds.

PERSONAL SAFETY

Anthony Burgess' *A Clockwork Orange* horrified people with its prospect of a future in which high tech could enrich the lives of so many, yet the society would polarize, spawning violent criminals and youth gangs. Many believe we have come face to face with that scenario, contributing to the intense fear of crime.

People see muggers, rapists and killers around every dark corner. Criminologists believe that fear of crime increasingly overlays the reality of it. As we all know, however, perception is reality. So Americans are arming themselves at an accelerating rate. Sales of mace, now legally sold in all 50 states, have increased 1000% in recent years. Bodyguard services for ordinary people, not just the rich, are springing up.

There is the growing feeling that government has failed to live up to its part of the social contract—to protect us. Consequently, because we elevate the importance of self, we are—and will go on—protecting ourselves. These efforts will range from more of us moving to walled enclaves protected by private security guards—to arming ourselves—to shopping at home. They will also include a trend toward inconspicuous consumption, such as wearing a Timex instead of a Rolex, or driving a less expensive car, so as to reduce one's chances of being targeted. The fear and anger felt about safety will derive to a considerable extent from the feeling that one's personal space and dignity become increasingly important at a time when individuals feel generally threatened by the vast social, technological, economic or natural forces for change they sense.

Some types of fears may not be real…some clearly will be troublesome. Scientists report that both the incidence and the catastrophic results of natural disasters are on the rise. According to a recent study by the UN, the number of people killed, injured or made homeless by natural disasters has increased an average of six percent a year over the last 30 years.

The alarm over gangs, which sometimes seems overblown, is actually justified. There are now more than 16,000 gangs in the U.S., and they have over half a million members. About 800 cities and towns now have gangs, up from 100 in 1970.

Other concerns may be based on perceptions more than on reality. FBI statistics show that reported crime, and in particular violent crime, has been declining for several years. Yet most people feel that crime is getting worse. This is largely because of the widespread perception that the violence attendant upon crime is becoming nastier and more irrational.

Disgruntled employees or ex-employees now too often kill not only their bosses but their co-workers. An American Management Association survey in 1994 reported that almost one-quarter of participating companies had at least one worker attacked or killed on the job since 1990. Another 31% reported threats of violence against workers. Domestic disputes now too often seem to end in murder. Robberies now seem to end more frequently in unprovoked killing. Indeed, some health authorities say we should classify violence as an epidemic and treat it as a public health issue.

A real factor in the coming violence issue is the projected increase in teenagers over the next 10 years. The percentage of the population aged 15 to 19 will increase by 21% by the year 2005. And we know that violence is committed disproportionately by young men in this age group. This factor is exacerbated by the increase in single parent households. Both boys and girls from such households are more likely to get in trouble than are those from two-parent families.

Another genuine challenge is the anticipated growth in terrorism. Ideological, cultural, religious and ethnic causes will generate an increase in violence aimed at what are called innocent parties. What will make all this frightening is a terrorist mindset that makes any and all human life meaningless when compared with the cause. As we get closer to the year 2000, millennialism may cause terrorist incidents to increase and to become more horrific.

As a result of all the real and perceived safety issues, and the fears they will generate, one of the fastest growing businesses in the future will be physical security. The U.S. market for private security services is expected to grow by about eight percent a year and will exceed $29 billion by the year 2000. More and more people are moving into private, walled communities. These communities customarily have gates as well as walls, electronic security systems, private police forces and even guard dogs.

Sales of home security services are also going up rapidly. Spending on such security systems amounted to approximately $10 billion in 1995. Already, almost one-third of all new homes are built with alarm systems. In stores and other businesses, more and more electronic security systems will be installed as well. Just one company that supplies such systems installed over 1000 hidden microphones in stores in a recent 12-month period. The private security guard business is now a $15 billion a year business. Private security personnel already outnumber police.

Eleven percent of American children now attend private schools, and this is becoming a booming business. Even in areas that are known to have good public schools, the percentage going to private schools—religious and secular—is surprisingly high, and getting higher. While much of this shift to private education will be driven by concern about the quality of education, there is no question that part of the motivation will be fear about children's safety.

CHAPTER 5

PERSONAL
SERVICE

At the turn of the last century, the servant class comprised the second largest employment category in the U.S. Much of the middle class had personal servants. Household help was not confined only to those with great wealth. Even those with rather modest means had one or two servants.

Industrialization brought education and better employment to greater numbers of working-class people, lifting them up into the higher wage and salary environments, making them shun servant work. Home appliances from vacuum cleaners to clothes washers replaced the time- and labor-intensive work of many household chores. Even the telephone made it less necessary to have servants, because messages could be carried by wire. Electric switches put energy at our disposal with a flick.

Now, as we approach the turn of another new century, we will see a return of personal service work. At the macro level, there will be a customization of formerly mass-produced goods and services. At the micro-level will be the rise of a new professional servant class.

Baby Boomers were weaned on the idea that they, as a group and individually, were at the center of the universe. Now, as adults, they form a massive market force demanding the personalized, customized, one-on-one services to which they feel entitled. With more women working and feeling short of time, and with the impacts of technology and more competition, innovative entrepreneurs will be happy to cash in on this trend.

MASS CUSTOMIZATION

Current examples of things to come—The Custom Foot is a shoe store where patrons have their feet electronically scanned. The data are transmitted directly to Italian factories, where the shoes are made to the exact customer specifications and measurement, and delivered in about two weeks, for a total cost of about $140.

A Japanese company, Paris Miki, digitally scans a face to produce a customized eyeglass lens shape that is more attractive for the wearer.

Levi's has begun selling made-to-order jeans for women by employing a personal computer recording the customer's relevant statistics, compiling a digital blueprint of the jeans, and transmitting this instantaneously to a factory in Tennessee, which prompts a robotic tailor to create the precisely custom-fit jeans. The cost is only about $10 more than ordinary retail, and the waiting time is about three weeks.

The price will come down because there are no costs of waste in this system—no wasted material, no inventory, no excess warehousing, no excess retail floor space, no excess transportation, no markdowns, no alterations. And the turnaround time will be much quicker. Eventually, combined with 3-D body scanning technology, CAD-CAM software will allow color, pattern, style and fabric to all be designed by the customer and produced on a custom-fit basis. In household design centers, auto dealerships and home-based food order systems, and just about everything else, the **Emotile Era** will see a rush of mass-customization. Marketing will shift from seeking customers for products to developing products for customers.

Customized packaging is no exception. Israel's Indigo Ltd. has its Omnius One-Shot printing system that makes it economical to print containers (labels, bottles, cans, boxes) in mini-lots, creating customized messages for special occasions. The School of Pharmacy at the University of London is among those developing capsules designed to customize the release of drugs. Their technology is based on pulses triggered electrically, timed to the individual body's biological clock.

Merck & Co. has placed a "virtual human resources" kiosk in 15 of its company locations, allowing its employees to choose from a menu of medical, dental, life, disability and other coverages. Signature Software, of Hood River, Oregon, introduced software that takes custom samples of handwriting and turns them into fonts for a computer, allowing computer-typed documents to be made in the typist's own penmanship. J. Edward Anderson of Boston University, working with Raytheon, is looking to commercialize the idea of personal rapid transit (PRT), which relies on small rail cars to carry up to four people who, as with a taxi, choose to ride together.

The factories that turn out customized products are themselves being reconfigured and customized. "Craftories," a new breed of craft-based business in a factory setting, are responding to the growing demand for individual craft products.

An IBM plant in North Carolina builds 12 products simultaneously by combining digital automation and human hands. The factory can customize products in quantities of *one* at mass-production speeds.

Cell manufacturing, where small teams of workers make entire products, is now in place in over half of all U.S.

factories, and 75% of those with over 100 employees use this approach. Not only does it speed up the process, reduce inventory and take up less floor space, but it also allows for the flexibility needed in custom production.

Malls are now targeted to specific ethnic groups. National chain stores are now micromarketing to local communities. Affinity clubs such as Harley-Davidson's Owners Group and Shiseido, Japan's largest cosmetics company, offer tailored group products, services and discounts to customers.

That's today. What of tomorrow?

As the target gets down to a unit of one—you, me—two major evolutions will take place.

First, advertisers will have to figure out how to better reach us. In a customized, pay-per-use world, ads will likely be more interactive, viewed at our request, and therefore be more substantive and entertaining.

Second, there will be the introduction of *more*, not fewer, agents and middlemen in the system. Why? Because the more providers go direct and customize, the more we will need informed intermediaries who can help us sort through the myriad choices. There is a mistaken assumption that more informed people are more effective consumers. Not necessarily. At least one study has shown that people with more education are more time- and convenience-constricted. Because their world gets more complex, they actually have less time to learn about their purchases. Thus, we will see more affinity groups acting as go-betweens.

PROFESSIONAL SERVANTS

Machines, we once believed, would free us of the need to spend so much time working. Some even forecast a 20-hour workweek. What there is instead is an increased workweek, particularly for managers and professionals—close to 45 hours a week on average in 1996. Even more important, there is substantial growth in the amount of time spent at work per household.

A major social and economic development of the last third of the 20th century has been the great increase in married women and mothers working full-time away from the home. Both spouses working full-time has subtracted considerably from the time available for household and family duties and activities. Even if the trend reverses, and more women remain home to raise their children, the great majority of women will do outside work of some kind during their lifetimes.

That one factor will be the major driver of the incredible growth in personal services.

Other trends, too, will help create the new professional servant class. Massive downsizings, layoffs and burnouts are leading well-educated, formerly high-wage earning individuals to shift careers, and many will choose to become creatively entrepreneurial in the service area. An important distinction—these people will view themselves not as servants, but as being "of service."

The number of options will overwhelm many people. Currently, we are ready to scream with impatience while the

TV Preview Channel scrolls down the listings for 50 or 75 cable station offerings. What happens when there are 500 stations? Or pay-per-anything (video or audio) ever recorded? When we can see, do or hear anything in the next hour, will we spend five hours reviewing our choices? No. More likely, we will have some personal entertainment agent—a software program or an individual—who knows us very well and who recommends our next hour's entertainment.

Personal workout trainers, personal chefs, personal financial advisers—there are no limits to the types of new services coming our way. Will this be an economy of each of us taking in each other's laundry and serving each other fast food? Not really. In the **Emotile Era**, one will be able to create a highly professionalized, independent, decent-paying *business* by doing a wide variety of things people want and need done for them.

One in six Americans hired someone to clean their home in 1994. That's up from about one in 10 in 1986. And almost 25% of Americans hire someone to do their yard work. More and more of the people who supply the services are better educated than their predecessors a century ago, and many take on the work because it provides tax-free (off-the-books) and independent income. Some turn their work into companies and become true entrepreneurs.

Some precursors: Capital Concierge sets up concierges in the lobbies of office buildings to provide personal and business services that range from picking up dry cleaning to overseeing a catered lunch. The National Restaurant Association says the fastest growing segment of the food market is "off premises," including catering and meal delivery.

There are 3,500 personal wardrobe consultants who work for Doncaster, one of the several women's clothing companies that sell by appointment only in the customer's own home. Doncaster's sales reached $50 million in 1995, up 14% over the previous year.

Thomas Leonard founded Coach University to take advantage of the burgeoning profession of "coaching"—a combination of consultant, therapist, friend, trainer, parent —all in one person who works with executives or entrepreneurs or professionals, or whoever, to get their lives on track. Coaches help people define their personal and/or professional goals, and then they help them achieve those. There are hundreds of coaches in practice now across the U.S. Their numbers are rising fast, and they get paid handsomely.

There is the "Barking Lot" van in Cambridge, Massachusetts, in which personal groomers go to their customers' driveways and bathe, brush and shave cats and dogs. The 100-seat Cinemobile in rural France delivers and features movies at $6.50 per person.

The One on One van in Chicago delivers a portable gym, complete with a Stair Master, treadmill, weights, TV and VCR, for $55 a session.

In New York, Mobile Psychological Services has four vans in which therapy is conducted on-the-go at $175 a session.

In Clarksville, Indiana, a woman gutted the rear of a 1954 fire truck and installed a swimming pool. She comes and gives children lessons—$30 for five classes.

While one man in California flies American men to Russia to find mates, another from Texas tracks down absentee parents and makes them pay child support. Some companies transport and care for children, some transport and care for the elderly.

The new professional servant class will continue to move rapidly in response to the middle class's need for time, convenience, intimacy, guidance, remote monitoring and home-based chores. Numbers are hard to come by, because many of these personal services entrepreneurs operate "off the books," and there is no agency officially cataloging their existence and growth. But we all know the practitioners—they are our former associates, our friends and neighbors, our parents and children, and ourselves. There is no question but that, combined with mass customization, personalized service will be a major component of the emerging **Emotile** economy.

CHAPTER 6

SPIRITUAL FULFILLMENT

Psychologists are familiar with Maslow's hierarchy of human needs. At the bottom are those things that assure basic survival, like food, shelter and clothing. At the top are those that lead to self-actualization—the full realization of one's potential. The **Emotile Era** will be about self-actualization, and a key component of it—spiritual fulfillment. In many different ways, through many different channels, people will seek out products and services, and systems and experiences, that satisfy their need for spiritual fulfillment.

But of all the areas of change we explore in this book, this is the hardest to analyze, because it presents a confusing and often contradictory mixture of trends and fads.

For example, there is a growing trend toward what has been called "voluntary simplicity"—giving up the pursuit of wealth and materialism in favor of focusing on finding a spiritual meaning in one's life.

At the same time, there is a trend toward materialistic indulgence, creating a luxurious home environment and spending lavishly on expensive foods, beverages and clothing.

DISCOVERY OF THE SELF

In November of 1995, Jeffrey E. Stiefler, president of American Express, announced that he was quitting his job so that he could "work at a less intense pace" and spend more time with his family. Here was a hard-driving, ambitious and hugely successful man who discovered that the real Jeffrey Stiefler was someone else, someone to whom making upward of $4 million a year was less important than watching his kids grow up.

What Stiefler did was not unique…only his prominence made it stand out. The fact is, many people will be making such decisions. Large numbers of executive women have been rethinking their careers—and choosing other paths. They are redefining themselves rather than retreating. That redefinition starts with the question: "Who do I really want to be?"

This search for identity is not new. Many of us remember all the young people in the 1960s and 1970s who went to Paris or Nepal or some other faraway place to "find themselves." What's new today is that it's not just young people now. More and more, it's people like Jeffrey Stiefler. So money is pouring into classes, seminars, books, programs, retreats and products that enhance our ability to "find" or "discover" ourselves.

And what will make it new tomorrow is the enabling factor of technology. Electronic networks will allow people to assume as many different identities as they want. A *New Yorker* cartoon depicts one dog at a computer talking to a dog lying on the floor and saying, "the great thing about the Internet is no one knows you're a dog." People will be able to form or join communities in cyberspace and use those nontraditional affinities to define who they are at any given time and in any given set of circumstances.

ETHNIC IDENTITY

For the last couple of decades, the hyphenated American has been a major trend. The primary determinant of one's identity has been the ethnic label—African-American, Italian-American, Mexican-American, etc. Many businesses have done well, and continue to flourish, by focusing on such ethnically defined market segments. The Greenbriar Mall in Atlanta, for example, caters exclusively to African-Americans.

But there are significant indicators of change here. Young new wave artists in California mix ethnic genres as a way of saying race doesn't matter. Young white teenagers are often "wannabes"—pretending to be Hispanic or black, even by changing their names.

More and more Americans, particularly young ones, will refuse to accept a hyphenated label and will call themselves "multiracial." Typical of these is the golfing phenomenon, Tiger Woods, who is of mixed Asian and black ancestry. He refuses to accept being labeled as one or the other.

Most important, assimilation, largely by way of intermarriage, is accelerating. Today in the U.S., only 20% of whites have spouses whose ethnic backgrounds match theirs. Among Italian-Americans and Polish-Americans, for example, upward of 75% marry outside their religion.

Almost 60% of Jews marry outside their religion. Less than two-thirds of Asians marry other Asians, and that figure is expected to change rapidly as these newcomer groups become Americanized. And the rate of black-white intermarriage is at least double what it was 10 years ago. So businesses that cater to ethnic tastes, clothing and traditions will thrive, as will those that cross-fertilize cultures. Just as new ethnic restaurants spring up in suburbs, so, too, will hip-hop and other crossover inner city fashions.

RELIGION

We are clearly entering the 21st century a more secular civilization than ever before. But when you monitor the media for signs of change, as we do, you sometimes see some striking things. One such thing recently is the great increase in media attention to religion. The *Dallas Morning News* has an entire weekly section on religion...ABC-TV has hired a religion reporter...National Public Radio and *The New York Times* have devoted increasing attention—including front page articles in the *Times*—to the subject.

Bookstores have given much more shelf space to books with religious themes as sales of such books have increased significantly in recent years. Sales of children's books with religious themes increased by more than 25% in the last couple of years. Angels and miracles are big, not only in books and periodicals, but in movies and on TV.

Religion in music, from pop to rap, is now seen as cool. DC Talk, a gospel rap group, sold over 800,000 copies of its debut album in 1994. Musicians and groups as diverse as U2, Bob Dylan, Peter Gabriel, John Mellencamp and Snoop Doggie Dogg are expressing spiritual themes and a search for eternal values.

Thousands of Jewish men and women are reasserting their religious identities through repeating coming of age ceremonies in midlife. A similar thing is happening among Southern Baptists, as people of all kinds become more concerned about their spiritual well-being.

One of the most striking aspects of this religious revival is the spread of Fundamentalism throughout the world. Strictly speaking, Fundamentalism is a phenomenon associated with American Protestants—a strict adherence to literal reading of Scriptures. But it has come to include the revolt against pure materialism and runaway modernity, and so it also fuels the spread of militant Islam.

Even the rise of conservative Judaism, and cults springing up around millennialism, attest to the desire of many to find some "fundamentals" that transcend the material world.

What it all amounts to is what Robert Fogel, professor of American Institutions at the University of Chicago, calls "the fourth great awakening"—an intensification of religious life, manifested in a focus on religion-based values as a basis for cultural reform.

As disillusionment with the modern world becomes more pervasive, it is no surprise that growing secularism will be met by the rise of a need for spiritual comfort. All major trends sow the seeds of their countertrends. To this end, many Baby Boomers will return to religion, although often not to the churches of their parents. And others will turn to New Agism, a more personal selection from cultural and belief systems and practices that break from Western tradition and dogma.

This revitalization of spirituality is likely to become more evident as the millennium draws nearer. Cartesian rationality may have run its course, for the time being at least. In its place will be a "post-scientific" culture based on feelings, faith and personal inner experiences—and all the products, services, businesses and jobs that will spring from these.

LEISURE

Here, too, paradoxes abound. More Americans are "cocooning," to use Faith Popcorn's term, isolating themselves and their families in today's counterpart of the walled, gated and moated castle of the past. This is facilitated by technologies that enable people to be entertained, fed and supplied entirely at home. Some authorities now see the home becoming not only the center of family life but the center of an immense market based on enhancing that life. Federated department stores reports that their home goods sales rose over 30% in just five years.

Over 70 million people spend time gardening in America, and they are increasingly moving from decorating their gardens with pink plastic flamingos to $1500 benches and $15,000 statues. The tabletop business—linens, glassware, china, etc.—is now a $60 billion dollar business as people are more concerned with the ambience of the home. There is a boom in very expensive home furnishings, such as 300-thread-count Egyptian cotton sheets.

Kathy Corey, author of *Rituals for the Bath*, sees the development of what she calls "the church of the bath"— making a luxurious experience out of taking a bath. And it is expected that by the year 2000, Americans will be spending more money on home renovation than on home construction.

On the other hand, despite predictions that telecommunications would shut down physical movement, overseas

59

trips by Americans went from 10.2 million to 14 million in the past two decades, and will continue to grow.

Libraries and museums are experiencing attendance booms. Fifty new science and technology museums have opened in the 1990s. Thirty-six new childrens' museums have come into being in the last five years.

The number of opera companies has grown from 60 to more than 100 in the last 20 years.

The cruise industry, though currently experiencing some woes, has seen the number of passengers go from 1.4 million in 1980 to five million in 1996...and further growth is coming.

What turns people on will continue to vary from person to person, and from age to age. But the merging of modern capacity with the age-old need for emotional release will see important new shifts in leisure businesses yet to come.

Edutainment will boom, more women will engage in once male-only activities (e.g., golf and backpacking), cyberspace will present us with virtual playgrounds and friends, and we'll see a surge in mythic stories that connect past with future.

Books, which help to slow down experiences in a fast-paced electronic world, will continue to exist, yet their geography-based sales sites, such as Barnes & Noble, will thrive on providing surrogate forms of community gathering places...rather than inventory and service as in the past.

And gambling will be a great boom business of the 1990s, with upward of $400 billion a year already being spent.

STEWARDSHIP

In the early 1960s, Harvey Cox, a professor of religion at Harvard and a leading liberal theologian, rewrote Genesis. He changed it from saying God gave man *Dominion* over the earth and everything on it (a hierarchical, exploitive model), to God gave man *Stewardship* for the earth (a caretaking role).

The new doctrine of Stewardship percolated for a few years and then began to seep through intellectual and religious circles. Its first area of impact was environmentalism. Coming at a time when many in the business community believed or hoped that environmentalism was a passing fad, it revitalized that movement. More important, it provided a powerful religious-moral underpinning. We now see environmentalism/stewardship entrenched in American values.

Up to three-quarters of all Americans regularly recycle. Only 10% did so in 1978. Religious institutions are increasingly involved in what has been called "the green church." They emphasize the stewardship responsibility to conserve, to recycle and to reduce pollution. Pollution abatement has now grown, by some estimates, to over 10% of Gross Domestic Product, when all industries, goods and services related to the environment are factored in.

Stewardship will spread to other spheres, as well. Community activity, for example. Young people are becoming increasingly active in volunteer community work. While younger people seem somewhat reluctant to be involved with large, established community organizations (they want to be more hands-on), these organizations, too, are seeing increased participation. About 90 million Americans, around half the adult population, volunteer at least three hours a week to nonprofit organizations. And there will continue to be a surge in growth of organizations promoting grass roots and local development and self-help, providing growing sources of community service jobs.

Women, who in past years were the main volunteers for charitable organizations, are now increasingly involved in other forms of community activity as well. Traditionally, women volunteered and men gave. Now women, who have more economic power, are giving as well as volunteering. And more and more they will be giving to, and volunteering for, organizations that advance their economic and political agendas. Emily's List, which backs pro-choice female candidates for office, is now America's third largest political action committee.

Political lobbying and activism around issues will be an increasingly powerful magnet for jobs and expansion of the economy.

And Stewardship will be more apparent in management theory and practice. Its current advocates range from Anita Roddick, founder of the Body Shop, to the dean of management consultants, Peter Drucker. The organization of the future, says Drucker, cannot be militaristically hierarchical but must be non-bureaucratic and based on the concept of human capital. The sense is growing that business will have to do more than make a profit—it will have to have a moral base that results in valuing people, protecting the environment and serving the community.

As Stewardship spreads even further in the years ahead, it seems likely to become one of the primary drivers of the new economic system that will undergird the **Emotile Era.**

CHAPTER 7

Ways of getting things done

Electronic technologies have burst inventiveness and creativity constraints. As a result, the world will be flooded with breakthroughs in the use of information, overwhelming barriers of time and space.

What's coming is the age of nanotechnology. "Nano" means "a billionth of." A nanometer is a billionth of a meter. A nanosecond is a billionth of a second. A nanometer is the size of a molecule. This is actually rather large, because quantum physics, a 20th century breakthrough, operates at the sub-atomic level. And a nanosecond is actually quite slow, since some scientists are working at the femtosecond level. A femtosecond is a millionth of a billionth of a second.

This will also be an age when traditional structural lines become less relevant, whether they divide company operations, lines of business, types of industries or even nation states. Connectedness will be expected, as the communications revolution spreads around the world.

It's no longer the big companies that consume the small. It's the fast that consume the slow. Speed will change the fundamentals of everything. AT&T's lasers will transmit information as light pulses through optical fibers that turn on and off 22.5 billion times a second. Soon it will be possible to transmit the equivalent of 600 volumes of the *Encyclopaedia Britannica* in one second...and we'll be going far beyond that.

Scientists around the world are developing quantum dots, wires and wells, in which single electrons are trapped, with the goal of building quantum-electronic computers that are a hundred times smaller than current models, and almost immeasurably faster.

DNA molecules are being harnessed to perform complex computations. Scientists are attempting to build and tailor proteins to carry out specific chemical tasks—in medicine, industry or environmental preservation.

Micromachines being developed at Sandia National Laboratories attain speeds of a half million rpm.

They will eventually revolutionize medicine, for example, as they become employed in unclogging arteries, destroying cancer cells, and helping to operate inside eyes and ears and inside the brain, too.

Genetically engineered bacteria in vats are being equipped with specially tailored genes that turn out designer proteins. This has already led to polymers that can serve as adhesive for living tissue, and "smart" plastics that respond to changes in their environment.

Inserting specially selected "foreign" genes into plants can create growing organisms that will produce desired by-products, such as pharmaceutical compounds, at prices never before possible.

The new economy will continually leverage the networking of human intelligence. Not only will people be better able to talk to each other, but so will "intelligent" computers. A "hypertext" world will emerge, encouraging formations of teams and cells that will continually innovate, further leveraging existing knowledge at a breathtaking pace. Within the next three decades, greater-than-human intelligence will likely occur through computer-human interfaces.

Materials that are smart, businesses and research conducted in space, earthquake- and weather-proof underground construction, infrastructures that are self-maintaining, intelligent transportation—all are on the drawing boards, all will make it into real life, our life.

Until now, laws and regulations regarding all these developments have lagged behind. Traditional law is based in geography, but the on-line networks don't exist in a fixed place. Lexis Counsel Connect, for a fee, provides an on-line meeting and working place for 35,000 member lawyers. Its founder also initiated the Virtual Magistrate pilot project, the goal of which is to offer a low-cost, fast, Net-based arbitration process for Net-specific issues.

With all of this change, values will be redefined. Free-flowing intellect and creativity will change the nature of who gets paid for what. Writers and artists, for example, would get paid for personally interacting with their audiences (in real time and space or in cyberspace), rather than for the content of their work, which will no longer be protectable.

Governments are clearly concerned about issues of tax revenue, as voice, image and data are transmitted electronically and all the taxable manual services that used to be employed in the publishing, replicating and delivering of these are swept aside.

The Information Society Project Office of the European Commission is studying how governments will be able to continue to raise funds in an increasingly information-based world in which value is generated through systems and global networks, rather than through clearly identifiable production and exchange.

An example of the challenge: An insurance company was just recently informed by its lawyers that, as the company's information traveled the globe from one point to another, anywhere along the way where it was parked in a country for "as long as a nanosecond" it could be subject to the laws and taxation of that country.

MANUFACTURING

Manufacturing strategy will soon be based on machines and materials that virtually make themselves. This self-assembly will be based on atoms, molecules, aggregates of molecules and components that arrange themselves according to their programming, without human intervention. Nanotechnology machines would be constructed by self-assembly. The ability to "grow" gold, or oil, or anything else, from the molecular level on up, is actually believed now to be possible. Alchemy ahead.

Already there is "desktop manufacturing." First came desktop publishing, which, via cheap computing and graphics, turned a mega-industry on its ear by allowing anyone to publish. Then came rapid prototyping and manufacturing (RPM).

One form of RPM is stereolithography. In this process, a vat is filled with a light-sensitive (photocurable) material—a liquid polymer or resin that hardens where and when exposed to light. A computer-programmed set of lasers slices through the material in nanometers (at the molecular level), based on a 3-D downloaded image of what the eventual manufactured part should be. Everywhere the lasers contact the material it hardens. In a few hours, the solid, manufactured object is pulled from the vat.

Currently, the material used in rapid prototyping is too resinous for mass manufacture, but progress is being made in the use of polycarbonates, a harder material. When that comes into use, much of the manufacturing world we know today will be a memory. So will all that goes with it: The smokestacks, the bricks and mortar, the amount of energy and people required, the warehousing, transportation and highway systems utilized—in the **Emotile Age**, the fixed and massive structures we have always associated with manufacturing will be increasingly irrelevant.

All over the world today various rapid prototyping techniques and computer-aided design (CAD) systems are being deployed.

Renault claimed in 1993 that its prototype car, the Racoon, was the world's first vehicle to be designed within the digitized world of virtual reality. Virtual reality allows architects, engineers, designers, or anyone, for that matter, to look inside, around, over, under or through anything, simple or complicated, as if it were real, except that it only exists in the computer. Researchers will "walk" inside molecules, architects will explore a building before a single brick has been laid down, interior designers will take customers through rooms to test the feel and placement of furniture that is not yet really there, and manufacturers will be able to build anything without a single real component.

For the first time, Boeing did not need to build a giant replica of its new 777 airliner to guarantee its component parts would fit together—its CAD System took care of that.

Detroit expects to employ virtual imaging technology to model prototype cars with "virtual clay."

In this book's earlier discussion of mass customization, we explored the ability of fashion companies and others to scan and relay personalized data to manufacturing facilities that will be able to cut, and even design, objects to special order as inexpensively as we once mass produced items in the Industrial Era.

Many former manufacturing companies will shift to marketing and services, and contract out their manufacturing. Contract manufacturers, now doing work that IBM, Intel, Hewlett-Packard and others used to do, are already doing in excess of $10 billion per year in the U.S. alone. We expect that to almost triple by 2000, a growth rate outpacing even that of computer, communications and electronics suppliers.

Dell, for example, buys circuit boards, disk drives and other modules designed for it, and has these assembled in warehouses.

Food and beverage companies will be increasingly creating and marketing products that are manufactured by other companies. In the pharmaceutical business, capacity unused because of inroads made by generics will increasingly be put to work in the manufacture of drugs for competitors.

Boundaries between and among competitors will become blurred as manufacturing creates overlapping relationships. With processes and technologies and production shared and resold, it will be hard to keep score the way we once did.

Outsourcing will produce "virtual" companies. What business will the virtual company be in? Integrating design with the customer's vision, cross-utilization of facilities, emphasis on marketing—all using computer-based networks— will lead to agility, mobility, flexibility and shifting alliances.

Small businesses will be as capable of playing in this game as the big boys. The global labor force, especially in engineering, will be brought into play. Singapore, Malaysia, Taiwan, India and Eastern Europe all have surpluses of engineering and scientific talent waiting to become employed in this networked environment. And the global corporations will be in and out of deals with each other opportunistically. New joint ventures, sometimes called "co-opetition," will pave the way for what author/consultant James Moore calls the "business ecosystem." He points out that it will sometimes be better to coevolve, rather than compete, with a rival.

Another interesting observation on manufacturing in the **Emotile Era**: A move to "never owned" products. Coming out of Europe, and catching on elsewhere in the world as a result of the sustainable development/ecological stewardship movement, will be the idea of leasing rather than owning items such as household appliances. People would buy functionality, rather than the item, while manufacturers would retain ownership and be accountable for recycling and responsibly disposing of the appliance later.

COMMUNICATING

The market for personal communications services (mobile and cellular phones) will explode around the globe. In less than a decade, we expect it to expand 200 times over, reaching $19 billion by 2002. Customers will be able not only to make and receive calls, but also transmit data and video while on land, water or in the air, anywhere in the world. One of the driving forces will be the **Emotile Era's** blurring of the boundaries between work, family, personal and professional lives.

Some analysts predict that, by 2000, 25% of American households will own a fax. HDTV (high definition TV) in digital format promises to deliver a whole range of extra services, such as on-line video, into the home well beyond what analog formats were capable of. Possible combinations of telephone, computer and cable will be explored on all fronts.

The communications revolution could lead to the demise of the corporate structure as we now know it. There could be, instead, single-function operations (all outsourced by a virtual organization) and/or individuals exchanging information at high speeds from anywhere to anywhere.

Politics will be transformed by the communications revolution. The beginnings: Britain, for example, has been experimenting with the uses of interactive cable technology by using its Channel 4's "People's Parliament" as a mock House of Commons in which randomly selected citizens debate and vote on controversial issues of the day. The White House and Congress have both reached out to the public on the Web.

The globe will be getting smaller as a result of the spreading network. In Latin America, consumers are more likely than those in the U.S. to say that the VCR, home computer, fax machine and answering machine are "necessities" rather than "luxuries." These ranked higher there than microwaves and dishwashers. Eventually, the fluidity of the Net will even affect Japan's rigid culture. China is fast coming on-line. Translation devices are being developed around the world for Chinese, Japanese, German, French, Spanish, etc.

Among the cultural shifts this **Emotile Era** of communications will usher in is how we say what we say—and to whom. The information overload we are now experiencing is leading to a social pressure to be succinct. As David Shenk says in *Wired*, those who are not economical about what they say, write or post on-line are "info-polluting."

Most of the business community prefers to meet face-to-face when giving detailed instructions or passing on motivational messages. UCLA research showed that the words we choose are only seven percent of how we communicate. Voice type accounts for another 38%, while body language, eye contact, posture and facial expressions account for 55%. All the technological advances of the coming age will not fully replace the need to really be there—at least from time to time.

This is important because we are often asked if the on-line world will replace existing media—newspapers, television, magazines, radio. Each medium has its own place and must find it to remain relevant.

When TV was first introduced, many believed that radio was finished. And it would have been if it hadn't gotten rid of its 20-piece orchestras, variety shows and murder mystery formats, all better done on TV. When radio finally found what it did best—talk, recorded music, news—it came back big time. Radio is currently integral to the socio-cultural and political life of the U.S.

The human brain processes information differently when exposed to on-line images vs. the printed page. Long-term memory is enhanced by co-location, which is to say that if we want to remember something we read in a newspaper last month, we are aided by remembering which section it was in, what ad was near it, where we were when we read it. It is difficult to do this as easily with on-line text, even if we print it out. Further, we cannot process large amounts of information at one time when it comes as pulsed images, because our brains get far more tired with this medium than with fixed images on a page. As long as magazines and newspapers relinquish timely reporting of statistics, outcomes and data to the electronic media, which do that faster and better, and they stick to context and depth, they will not die out. But the new electronic competition will demand that they be nimble, relevant and capable of truly delivering.

WORKING

The wired, networked organization will challenge hierarchy, autonomy, decision-making and turf. Access to information will become decentralized, executives will all learn the keyboard (until voice recognition devices take over), and boundaries of time and place will be ignored as teams work from anywhere at any time.

Many executives have become computer-literate, but not many are information-literate—they know how to find the information but they don't know how to leverage it. Peter Drucker recognizes that organizations need organized information, and that information should be challenging what is currently assumed. But it is hard for most of those already in senior positions to relinquish control to a more amorphous, knowledge-intensive quasi-organization.

The futurist founders of the French think tank Prometheus observe that most of what is called information technology today is now relationship technology, and relationships everywhere, especially in the workplace, are in change.

The giant Swiss-Swedish company Asea Brown Boveri (ABB) has a board of eight directors with four different nationalities and an executive committee of eight people from five countries. English is its corporate language. Financial results are reported in dollars. Few corporate boards today are this tolerant of different or culturally diverse perspectives, but the organization of the future will have to be. Diversified workforces will have to be motivated toward a common purpose to succeed in the **Emotile Era**.

Making money will become the responsibility of *everyone* in the organization. Reflecting this, companies will increasingly tie pay to performance, forcing people to see beyond their immediate job and to look at the goals of the organization. This, in turn, will require the organization to reorder work and information flow so that each employee has the tools to achieve this.

The recent spate of re-engineerings has met with a few qualified successes and many dismal failures. Perhaps this is because most restructuring was done not to get "from here to there" but "from here to anyplace else, preferably somewhere that someone else has gotten to successfully." Creating waves of backlash, most organizations who re-engineered and restructured are left with the walking wounded—demoralized people who feel guilt for having their job while others were let go. They do not know for whom they are working—or for how long. They see projects they put long hours into get thrown into the scrap heap, and they are told they are empowered only to learn that they are afraid more than ever of the pink slip.

Into this chaos came TQM—the Total Quality Management movement. It is no surprise that the movement is in trouble. It was the product of a top-down, hierarchical, "Dominion" era, but something profoundly different will govern work as we move into the 21st century.

As we point out in Chapter 6, *Stewardship* (responsibility for the world) is coming to replace *Dominion* (rule over the world) in our value system. This shift in view has the potential to change work life forever.

Quality is a concept that grows out of Dominion—the hierarchical command that is given from top down to organize for the benefit of satisfying the customer at all costs. Usually that means at all costs to the employee, through job-cutting, overwork, strangled budgets, declining morale and chaos.

The Stewardship concept that would underlie *revisioning* (a stage that *must* precede reengineering) is not quality, but *integrity*— open, honest and fair dealings with all one's stakeholders, but in *particular* one's own people. If integrity underpins the organization, and people really do come first, the customer will be well served automatically, because the employee's goals are aligned with the company's and no energy is wasted in constantly propping up an artificial system of morale.

A comparison of how the two values lead to different organizational outcomes:

Dominion	*Stewardship*
•Hierarchical	•Horizontal
•Exploitive	•Caretaker
•Quality: Customer First	•Integrity: One's People First
•Employee uncertainty— quality breaks down	•Employee alignment— quality a natural by-product

Work teams will continue to proliferate and grow, but they will function best in those companies where the workers (employees or independent contractors or strategic allies) have faith in the integrity of the new system. These same teams will fail in those companies that are stuck in the Dominion model of the Industrial Era.

Flexible work hours and workweeks will become more common, as will flexible cafeteria-style benefits packages. Vacations may increasingly be taken in hours rather than days. Workers will be asked to manage their own careers, allocate, determine and invest their own pension funds, select their own healthcare, and choose between working part-time or full-time. Temporary work will boom, and it will spread among professionals. This again will be out of both necessity and choice. Contractual employment will move down in the organizational ranks. Casual clothing will continue to move into the workplace, as work stations move into the home.

All sorts of barriers will fall. The physically challenged will be augmented by technology in wondrous ways, with aids for the sight-impaired and hearing-impaired and even interfaces that allow those who are paralyzed to use their thoughts to control computers. Ergonomics, the science of suiting the work environment to the human form and function, will gain ground.

Work-family balance is now in the spotlight, and will remain so. In the **Emotile Era**, personal fulfillment and sound mental health will be highly esteemed goals. Workers who are now constantly in touch with co-workers and clients via portable computers, faxes, phones and beepers will come to value privacy by disconnecting from time to time. The glitz and status associated with high-tech portability and connectedness will eventually fade as it all comes to be taken for granted, and real status will accrue to those who can select the time when they are unreachable. Urban dwellers will take to rural communities and be just as connected as if in town. Geography will blur—rural, urban and suburbia all will become "rurbania."

And automating, too, will go on. Farmers will make more use of robots—machines that can plant and harvest crops. Highways and roads will be worked on by robot repair crews. The Dutch have deployed a multimedia system that puts computers on street corners to do the routine, information handling work of police officers, with input directly by citizens. The Florida Highway Patrol is augmented by the state's one million cellular telephone users who spot drunk and reckless drivers.

William Calvin, a neurophysiologist at the University of Washington, sees computers soon taking on more human-like qualities, ushering in the "workalike," which will begin to displace higher educated workers.

In Australia, engineers are outfitting robots with their own "pheromones," equipping them to "spit out," detect and follow a trail of camphor so they can mark territory and find their way home. A company called Photomic Sensor Systems is working with the Georgia Institute of Technology to develop microsensors that will diagnose specific diseases, pollutants or fertilizer imbalances. The British company Neotronics has developed the first artificial nose, with only 12 sensors as opposed to the human's 10,000. It can be adapted for work in any industry whose products or processes depend on smells, vapors or gases. And elsewhere scientists are trying to strengthen the immune systems of computers to help them ward off viruses.

Lightweight, rechargeable batteries, organic materials, solar energy and superconductivity will make headlines in the energy sphere. Work is use of energy, and these, like all the other developments in this chapter, hold out the promise of work done smaller, easier, cheaper and more decentralized.

DISTRIBUTION

Disintermediation is a term that cropped up in the late 1950s to label what was happening as more people took their money out of banks and shopped around for higher rates of return elsewhere. This changed the role of the traditional savings intermediary and created a whole new universe of financial services. The term has since come to apply to the bypassing of traditional delivery channels for all goods and services in the economy.

Many middlemen have been erased, new ones have been added, and businesses have gotten into different businesses where they can apply their core competencies. Circuit City uses its retailing ability to sell cars. Shell Oil is the largest seller of packaged sausages in Scandinavia.

Just as the telephone monopoly was disbanded, the electric utilities, too, have clearly begun to be disintermediated. Customers, large and small, will be free to shop for electricity anywhere. Utilities' growing ability to transmit information as well as kilowatts could eventually put them into the electronic shopping and entertainment businesses. And customers who generate energy or buy excess energy will themselves become competitors in the sale of electricity to others.

Affinity groups and wholesale clubs will become very important distribution channels, creating network-based deal making and purchases. Small companies are aggregating into chains. Category-killer stores, such as CompUSA and Home Depot, are not only focusing on greater selection and low cost, but all the peripheral services as well. And more companies will be buying or providing catalog or on-line shopping services to avoid losing customers. As virtual reality technology gets further along, this on-line shopping experience will become even more attractive.

But in-person shopping will not disappear. And Main Street will make a comeback even as malls struggle to regain their footing. Real sites will still have a place for those who marry them with one or more trends that make them relevant.

For example, the biggest on-line sales company is one that sells books, yet Barnes & Noble is flourishing. That is because both will fit into the **Emotile Era**. Barnes & Noble is successful not merely because it sells books, or because it has a big selection, but because it provides a wonderful place for people to *be*, especially the growing numbers of people, uprooted from their birth community, who often find themselves alone. These people may want to be *left* alone, but they don't want to *be* alone. Companies such as Barnes & Noble and Starbucks will make money delivering community through the marketplace. And these companies and others like them will, at the same time, become more aggressive on-line.

It is important to recognize that as the future unfolds, the greatest story in delivery channels will be *more options*. Not absolute replacement, but choices. Around the world, on-site retailing is booming, on-line retailing is booming, catalog shopping is booming, direct selling is booming.

The real losers in the future will be those whose skills are outdated, and whose delivery systems have not been revamped to meet the new competition. This is more descriptive of some of the purveyors of professional services than of sellers of goods. What will happen if computers may be able to better predict than doctors whether someone has prostate cancer, robots may be better able to perform brain surgery, data systems may better help patients treat themselves, and health monitoring may be better performed remotely by a doctor hundreds of miles away than one nearby?

Software programs are already displacing the work of some traditional accounting services. Do-it-yourself programs and paraprofessionals are taking over some of the practices of the legal professional, such as wills and divorces. This defrocking of the professional priesthoods is one of the major shifts of our time.

And so, as each profession is faced with the need to reconceptualize itself...big changes lie ahead...

CHAPTER 8

Ways of

Building

Relationships

One important point that seems to get lost in the many disputes about how technology will change our ways of life is that human needs change very slowly, if at all. The very human needs for family, companionship and community will endure. What will change is how we create the relationships and how we maintain them. The new technologies are adding another dimension to how people form relationships. This new dimension increases our choices and decreases our limits.

FAMILY AND HOUSEHOLD

We constantly remind our clients that they should avoid putting negative labels on trends and events. To do so is an act of prejudgment. It results in limiting one's ability to fully understand what will happen and to find ways to benefit from it. One of the most commonly applied pejoratives is "the decline of." The most common usage is "the decline (or deterioration) of the traditional family."

When we ask what is meant by the term "the traditional family," most people describe what social scientists call the nuclear family—a father who goes to work and a mother who stays home to take care of the children. But this so-called traditional family is an artifact of the 20th century. It is the family form that evolved to fit into an industrialized society, dominated by the motor vehicle. Before that, the traditional family was the extended family, comprising several generations, with most women working, often on the land or as shopkeepers, seamstresses, whatever. And before that it was the clan.

In truth, the family, like all social institutions, adapts to fit its circumstances. Urbanization, mobility and the increased independence of women transformed the family from an institution based primarily on law and custom to one based essentially on love and companionship.

Trends in the late 20th century have furthered that transformation. One of the most important factors is the blurring of the customary gender-based division of labor in the family. For example, by 1960, 19% of women with children under the age of five were employed outside the home. In 1995, that number was 55%. This reduction of female economic dependency on men invalidated the traditional arrangement—men providing financial support in exchange for domestic services from women.

In a somewhat plaintive cover story, *U.S. News and World Report* said that men's productive and reproductive roles are diminishing. Anthropologist Lionel Tiger blames all this on the pill, which, he says, emancipated women and reduced men's "paternity certainty." On the other hand, a recent study by the Population Reference Bureau sees signs in the late 1990s of a stabilization in the family situation. According to that study, there has been a recent increase in the number of two-parent households with children, and the divorce rate seems to have plateaued and even diminished a little.

What it appears will happen, if we don't let labels interfere with our vision, is a reaffirmation of the family *function* even as the family *structure* will change. One emerging phenomenon is the "intentional family," in which unrelated people get together for holidays, birthdays and other family-type occasions.

A related development, epitomized by Hillary Rodham Clinton's book, *It Takes a Village*, is the growing emphasis on a wider sharing of responsibility for the well-being of children—almost a return to the clan form of family. Social scientists are predicting the growth of "para-parenting," relationships in which adults other than the mother and father take on some responsibility for the children. These other adults might be grandparents or other relatives, or they might be godparents, or mentors, or friends or even neighbors.

And we're also seeing the extended family reemerging. Travel agents are expecting a further increase in vacation trips, including cruises, in which parents and children are joined by one or more grandparents. A recent Atlas Van Line survey reported that concern about the care of an aged parent was the primary reason given by 64% of employees for rejecting relocation. The job of the spouse came in second.

We're also projecting the growth of another kind of family—the *multinational* family. This is a family in which one or more members reside in another country, earning money there and sending part of it to where the rest of the family lives.

What it all amounts to is that yes, the family will change, but that's not necessarily bad. There's overwhelming evidence that family matters very much to people. Homosexuals want to be able to live in family situations. Young people who might otherwise have chosen to live together are deciding instead to engage in "starter marriages."

Technology is not likely to alter the fundamental human need for family. What does seem likely is that we will have several, rather than one, preferred family models. There will also be a much higher degree of impermanence. People will move from one model to another, from one relationship to another, much as they will move from one job or career to another. Temporariness will lose the stigma it has had.

FRIENDS AND COMMUNITY

New developments in technology will increasingly enable people to become members of "virtual" communities. These communities, unlike those we now know, are not determined or defined by location. Instead, they will be defined by commonality of interest. Communicating through networks, people will identify and associate with people who share their interests, their ethnicity, their problems, their "workplace," their religion or philosophy, whatever. A glimpse of things to come appears in the report of a young hacker, dying of cancer, who brought his computer and modem to the hospital so that, as he said, "I can die among my friends."

It will soon be possible for people to have available to them personal telephone numbers, which could be theirs for life and which could move with them wherever they go. This could be resisted, however, for privacy considerations. Symbolically as well as really, this represents another breaking of the ties between people and places. Technological developments like beepers, mobile telephones, modems and portable computers, will all lead to the possibility of a complete severance of our place-based bonds.

In 1995, Harvard professor Robert Putnam published an essay that created a stir in intellectual circles. Titled "Bowling Alone: America's Declining Social Capital," the essay contended, based on a 40% decrease in league bowling between 1980 and 1993, that community participation was deteriorating because Americans were increasingly less civic-minded. But Putnam may have been looking in the wrong places. Although league bowling was down, all bowling had an increase of 10% during that period. And nobody bowls alone.

And while some civic participation showed a decline, other forms continue to rise. PTA membership is increasing significantly. Union membership is rising. Voter turnout in 1992 and 1994 was the highest in 20 years, although it declined in 1996. Youth soccer leagues now have two and a half million participants, up from a little over 100,000 20 years ago. Charitable contributions, totaling $16 billion in 1970, are now well over $100 billion a year.

What is happening is that the nature of participation is changing. Civic involvement will no more stay static than will any other social institution. Men don't join the Shriners or the Elks the way they used to. But Promise Keepers, a nondenominational religious organization for men, has grown in a few short years to over three-quarters of a million participants.

Most significantly, we are seeing the rise of community associations. These are associations of homeowners and of neighborhood merchants that serve in a quasi-governmental capacity, except that they are bottom-up rather than top-down. They make rules and provide services intended to enhance the quality of community life. There were 10,000 such associations in 1970. As we head toward the 21st century, there are already more than 150,000.

The cyberspace community, in which individuals elect to participate on the basis of shared interests or values, will be a radical change from the traditional community based on geography. There will be "intentional" communities—as opposed to "accidental" ones —in which people who have values, religious beliefs or political ideologies in common and live near each other create a kind of gerrymandered neighborhood.

Reunions will continue to be very big. Even now, there are about 150,000 school reunions every year, and 200,000 family reunions. There are also about 20,000 ex- or retired employee reunions each year. The ideal of community is not dead in America.

Then there is the commercialization of relationships and community. Entrepreneurs, professionals and marketers will turn community into a marketable commodity. Early examples include...

- An Atlanta-based entrepreneur, Mike Correll, has built a thriving business on the premise that successful men don't have enough time to make friends, but they have enough money to buy them. So he matches such executives— over 1,000 so far—with people with whom they can be friends, for a $1,200 fee.

- An organization called Institute for Community Design Analysis helps existing towns and cities re-make themselves into idealized communities. They create "defensible space," whereby walls, lighting, fencing, shrubbery and traffic patterns are used to fashion a safe neighborhood.

- New towns—such as Seaside in Florida and Kentlands in Maryland—are manufactured to re-create the old-fashioned neighborhood.

- Religious institutions are focusing on community, too. The so-called megachurches offer not only worship but shopping, exercise and social activities and affiliations of merchants who share their beliefs.

And we are seeing major changes in our larger communities as well. Richard Rosecrance, writing in *Foreign Affairs*, describes the coming of the virtual state. Such a state will be downsized in terms of its functions, because geography has become less important than economic efficiency. A virtual state will outsource some functions and concentrate its resources on those activities that give it competitive advantage.

A striking recent forerunner of the virtual state, interestingly enough, comes not from the developed world but from the developing one. Eritrea, in east Africa, is instituting a new constitution that was created by expatriate Eritreans around the world who created a parallel country, Dehai, in cyberspace and wrote the constitution for it.

Eritreans on the Internet pondered and wrote rules governing such issues as the role of religion, how religious freedom will be guaranteed and how women's rights will be assured.

PROFESSIONAL AND CORPORATE RELATIONSHIPS

It has been obvious for several years now that the world of organizations, for-profit and not-for-profit, has been going through wrenching change. As in all previous times of transition in human history, technology is revolutionizing how work is done. And as in all previous times, when machines get cheaper than people, they replace people.

The big difference in today's displacement is that previous technologies—the gun, the plow, the wheel—amplified or replaced human muscle. The computer amplifies or replaces human brains. And so the service sector of our economy, which is made up largely of knowledge workers and which accounts for 75% of the workforce, is now being mechanized. The critical event occurred in January of 1994, when the Xerox Corporation, coming off the best year in its history, announced that it was cutting its workforce by 10%. This meant that henceforth companies in the service sector would reduce their workforces not because they had to, but because they could.

The old relationship between employers and employees, as a result, will be fundamentally changed. That old relationship was based on mutual loyalty, paternalism and permanence. The new relationship will be based on pragmatism rather than loyalty, on individual self-reliance rather than paternalism and on impermanence. Employees will be in charge of their own lives and careers.

More organizations will look to temporary alliances rather than internal growth. Competitors, as in the telephone business, will ally to get a contract or accomplish a job too big for any one company. Companies will also look to establish closer and longer-lasting relationships with suppliers and distributors on the grounds that this will enable them all to control costs and to maintain quality.

These and other changes will force new ideas of organization. The strategy-structure-systems management model of the 20th century won't do anymore. Organizations will come to depend on the unique qualities and abilities of individuals who can add value to information, and so will move to an entrepreneurial and people-centered model. This will mean a shift away from control systems and toward facilitation systems.

All these changes will call for the entrepreneurial individual, whether as an employee or a business owner. Since Pepsico announced in 1989 that it was making stock options available to all employees, more than 2,000 companies have done the same. The comfort that comes from knowing that one can have a secure and long-lasting job will be replaced by the uncertainty of an equity stake in one's self and one's company.

We can all remember when we would travel to professional or business conferences and we would meet new people, network and collect business cards. We'd put these in our Rolodex, and six months later we could call the number on the card and catch up with that person. No more. Probably half the people we meet are not at the same work number six months later. Whether across professions or businesses, we find ourselves not able to count on anyone being where they were, doing what they were, or even being interested in the same things, when next we see or hear from them. All of our individual working relationships will continue to be constantly challenged.

The same is true for many trade and professional groups. The slower moving societies and associations around which professional practitioners come together for their common good are becoming less effective as members focus less on common interests and more on self-interest. The more nimble associations will survive and thrive. Here, too, technology will enable change. Dissident members, often younger, will be able to form ad hoc associations in cyberspace that will drain energy from —and often work against—established institutions. New networks will spring up, and they will be flexible, responsive and highly **Emotile**.

AND SO...

In the 1970s and 1980s, many people found themselves going through transitions. The lock-step life cycle of the past was no longer a straight line for them...it was jagged and zig-zag. They found themselves changing not only jobs but careers. They found themselves with disruptions and resumptions of family life. Life became fragmented rather than whole.

What will be happening into the 21st century is the next step in that process. It's what we call transitioning. That is, life is not just a series of episodic transitions. It is one long state of transition, a condition of permanent impermanence. People will never be quite sure of where they are at any given point, of how long they will be there, or of where they will be next.

We will all be nomads in our minds. While this can make people feel dispensable, that is the negative perspective. A more positive outlook would be that it can transform people into masters of their own destiny, making their lives less subject to blind fate or the whims of others.

It has reached the point where the eminent psychiatrist, Robert Jay Lifton, in his book, *The Protean Self*, proclaims that the changeable, multi-personality individual will be the one best equipped to cope with tomorrow's rapidly changing world. Not too long ago, most therapists believed that such an individual was unhealthy and needed treatment. It brings to mind the immortal words of country singer Waylon Jennings: "I've always been crazy, but it's kept me from going insane."

CHAPTER 9

Ways of

Viewing

The World

I t is as if all of us are Alice entering the looking glass.
We are bemused by the revival of small towns and rural
areas, by the splitting of the middle class into the con-
fident "know-mores" and the anxious "know-lesses," by a
newly skilled, well-paid and smaller "blue-collar" class, by
dispersed global production along with great concentrations
of global power, by society arranging itself in networks
rather than in neighborhoods, by money traders and fund
managers replacing bankers (and even governments), by the
declining percentage of men as primary breadwinners, by

customers and constituents wresting power away from the controlling institutions.

Some observers see in all this a shift away from scientists, technologists and other rationalists. Vaclav Havel, President of the Czech Republic—and playwright—was right. "In this time of post-modernism, everything is possible and almost nothing is certain."

We are moving more and more into the age of "derivativity"—toward virtual dimensions that define reality. Wealth used to be concrete—land and bricks and coins. Then it became abstract—paper money and letters of credit. And then it moved further along this abstract road to equities and bonds—to bundled instruments —to options—to hedging instruments. In the process, we have been moving further from what we could see and touch, and into the realm of wealth through conjecture. So, too, will abstraction or derivativity be injected into all of our other levels of meaning.

In culture and the arts, hype will rule and interactivity will allow the viewer to be the creator. Cities will exist in cyberspace. Enchantment with magic and extraterrestrial life will abound.

In business and commercial transactions, the workplace will be mobile and digitized, chaos theory and particle science will be applied to Wall Street. Digital cash and global shopping malls will emerge. The "non-real" world of entertainment will provide the technology by which business and the military create breakthroughs.

"Smart" fabrics will become extensions of your own body. You will enter virtual worlds and become whomever you please, and you will be able to alter your brain by what you eat and drink.

"Morphing," the blending and distorting of images, will actually come to describe our worldview. While historians talk about the coming clash of cultures, cultures will be merging and blurring as much as becoming hard-edged and distinct. Eastern and Western scientists will combine scientific viewpoints and philosophies as they work together over global networks. Technologies will overlap.

Scientists will increasingly be asked to address the social, moral and legal implications of their work. Quantum physicists will work on proving paranormal events, as they come to believe that bends in the space/time continuum allow subatomic particles to travel backward and forward in time, and people can perceive these even though they cannot repeat the experience in traditional laboratory tests.

Scientists will feel more comfortable embracing religion, because the idea is that, if we must increasingly take new science on faith, then we can certainly accept religion on faith. More scholars are already studying religion and science together, focusing on the overlap between the two.

THE TRANSCENDENTAL

The central banks of nations around the world have had to shift their focus from domestic to global money supplies. Currency transfer has become the largest daily dollar volume business—over $1.3 trillion* a day in 1996—and the global movement of dollars is one indication of the waning power of national governments. The balance of power in marketing, media, information, entertainment, culture and environmental concerns will shift away from territorially-bound governments to global networks, including global corporations—and global affinity groups, such as the Nation of Islam or Evangelical Protestantism. What will be sold and bought, believed and dreamt, worked on or traded, will transcend the old boundaries.

The network configuration is taking hold as a metaphor for the coming age. As Kevin Kelly, in *Out of Control: The Rise of the Neo-Biological Civilization*, puts it, "It is a bunch of dots connected to other dots, a cobweb of arrows pouring into one another...the restless image fading at indeterminate edges." No beginning, no end, no center. Author Gregory Stock says our worldwide human activities are now collecting into an unprecedented, potent organism, "Metaman"—growing at an exponential rate, and evolving from decisions made on the basis of massive data banks of collected thought.

Areas of study are transcending their original disciplinary walls. Biology is merging with physics and chemistry, anthropology leans on materials science and feminist stud-

*To gain perspective on this number, let's assume we counted out one dollar every second. Consider that one day has about 86,000 seconds. One billion seconds would take about 32 years, and one trillion seconds almost 32,000 years.

ies, economics is overlapping with psychology and ecology. All this is leading to the exercise of "thinking about thinking," the actual title of a popular new Harvard course jointly taught by lawyer Alan Dershowitz, paleontologist Stephen Jay Gould and philosopher Robert Nozick.

Within the corporation, problems are decreasingly compartmentalized as "accounting," "finance," "systems," "human resources," "marketing," "planning" or "administration." Developments such as teleconferencing and E-mail will accelerate communication, causing knowledge to spill over traditional boundaries, creating new investigative tools that allow the asking of new questions.

THE RELATIVISTIC

Within this morphed and transcendental world, absolutes will be harder to come by. While many people and institutions would like to steer the public to clearcut choices of morality and values, people will increasingly become citizens of nowhere in particular, having to learn to adapt to the ambiguity that comes with divided sovereignty and multiply-situated selves.

Futurist Walter Truett Anderson points out that we're moving from "found" (socially imposed) identities to "made" identities (self-determined), from "found" single-cultural moorings to "made" morality forged out of dialogue and choice.

We are heading toward art and culture in which no style dominates, but in which we are offered endless improvisation and variation, and into a globalization in which people view man-made borders as artificial constructions and feel free to cross them, erase them or reconstruct them.

Some believe this persistent move leads to a fragmented sense of time, reduced attention span and a general lack of patience for long or sustained inquiry. Others see it as erasing all sense of "real." Digital software programs enable dead celebrities to be resurrected in TV commercials, photos to be re-imaged, black and white footage to be colorized, people to be projected into virtual worlds, and dinosaur DNA to be extracted and reconstructed.

Artificial life, not just artificial intelligence, is part of the new realm of postmodern science, in which digitized creatures are evolved and infused with human qualities. Works of art can be perfectly synthesized, leaving even the experts to question which one is "real." The same can be said for humans in the age of cloning. Computers can bring dead singers back to the microphone and even create duets with them, and symphonies can be constructed from the most perfect notes of a piece recorded anywhere combined into one rendering of the piece.

Where children once played with historically and culturally representative toys, increasingly their games and toys reflect the extraterrestrial, the transformational, the multicultural, the disconnected.

CHAPTER 10

OUR PERSPECTIVE ACROSS THE FOUR AGES

This brief introduction to the next era cannot fully describe the complex forces leading us there or the dynamic and exciting aspects of the coming age. For example, take the concept of time.

In the Agricultural Era, nature dictated time and people did everything (work, celebrate, sleep) based upon day and night and seasons. When clocks were introduced in the early stage of the Industrial Era, there were hardly any around. Some enterprising fellow might have jumped on a horse, ridden through town, and called, "Eleven o'clock and all is well!" Never, "Eleven ten" or, "Eleven twenty-three," because hardly anyone even cared that it was eleven. But then when people had to go to work, take lunch breaks, and be subjected to time and motion studies, hours, minutes and even seconds became important, and the clock (and watch) more ubiquitous.

The Post-Industrial Era introduced computers and digital time, enabling us to measure time in fractions of a second. Has this made a difference in society? Well, there could not have been the 1994 Winter Olympics 40 years ago, because there would have been several competitors tying in such major events as downhill skiing, bobsledding and speedskating. But because speed in sports can now be measured to fractions of seconds, the materials industry innovated and changed the nature of equipment and clothing to capitalize on that. Sports medicine was introduced to deal with the body as a machine and fine-tune it to perform to fractions of a second differences. And about 15% of all U.S. high school athletes took steroids in order to engineer improvements, even in minute degrees, of performance.

As we move into the **Emotile Era**, time will lose a great deal of its meaning. We will no longer be forced to live in lock-step patterns. We can each work, be entertained, sleep, transmit business, whatever, at our own convenience.

There is one value time will have that it never did before—its role in the value of information. In the **Emotile Era**, information (knowledge), our greatest economic asset, will have a time value such that some information can be worth *billions* of dollars the moment it's generated (e.g., a change in the currency exchange rate) and *nothing* moments later! We have never had an asset that behaved that way in any former economy. (Some telephone companies are still depreciating copper cable!) And a nanosecond age would render some processes, such as currency trading, too fast for the human brain, thus requiring that people who are now considered highly skilled be replaced by machines.

The following grid summarizes the **Emotile Era** transformation. It will give you an idea of how one dozen societal underpinnings are fundamentally transformed each time society adapts to its economic realities.

THE FOUR AGES: A SAMPLING OF

AGRICULTURAL	INDUSTRIAL

1. Time

Seasonal, calendar time structured people's lives.

People begin to structure time, clocks, workweeks, shifts.

2. Household

Extended family, tied to the land, rural, self-employed in family enterprise or in service to a single land-owner.

Decline of extended family (beginning of nuclear family), tied to urban employer(s), women who didn't have to work, rise of concept of male breadwinner.

3. Education

One-room, up until teen years, apprenticeships.

Neighborhood schools, age cohorts, vocational training, attendance and age mandates, strengthened uniform public education.

4. Health

Rule of nature over humankind, hands-on delivery.

Application of science to temper nature, professional delivery.

5. Wealth

Farmland (real assets), many sons.

Large home, capital assets, community respect, savings and pensions (Protestant Ethic).

6. Success

To own one's own property, to have more than it takes to feed one's own family.

To own one's own business, to build wealth.

DISTINGUISHING CHARACTERISTICS

POST-INDUSTRIAL	EMOTILE
Partial triumph over nature (crop growth, 24-hour society), computers and digital timepieces measure in thousandths of seconds, time becomes desired commodity, speeds up.	Instant, programmable (VCRs, microwaves, genetic engineering, 24-hour global immediacy), time irrelevant to access, too fast for humans.
Nuclear family, suburbia, two-income households, serial family formation (divorce, stepchildren), commuter marriages.	Family constantly redefined, non-fixed households, multi-residence, multi-national. Merger of home and office.
Higher education, pre-school, adult education, credentialism, democratization of all public education processes, weakened public school system.	Electronic, life-long, knowledge haves and have-nots.
Life extension, control over nature, institutional delivery.	Control of, and creation of, nature itself, genetic engineering, brain mapping, cybernetics, remote monitoring.
Large income, access to credit, many material possessions.	Financial security individually determined, emotional and physical well-being, access to and knowledge of how to manipulate information.
To master the skills of a profession or career and spend wealth.	To be self-sustaining and safe, to amass a wealth of experiences, to have frequently reinvented oneself.

THE FOUR AGES: A SAMPLING OF

AGRICULTURAL	INDUSTRIAL
7. Energy	
Manual, wind.	Steam, gas, electric.
8. "The Boss"	
The father, the owner-farmer.	The entrepreneur, the capitalist.
9. Retirement	
Not a factor.	Set at 65, thought to precede death by only a few years.
10. Assets of Enterprise	
Livestock, farmable real estate, equipment, water.	Machinery, buildable real estate, monetary capital, access to markets.
11. Weapons of Warfare	
Axes, guns, arrows, fire, hand-to-hand combat, boats.	Tanks, mines, planes, bombs, more sophisticated guns, warships, chemicals.
12. Science	
Flat-earth, humans at center of universe, deterministic.	Copernican, Jungian/Freudian, Newtonian (mechanistic), heuristic.

DISTINGUISHING CHARACTERISTICS

POST-INDUSTRIAL	EMOTILE
Electric from numerous sources, nuclear.	Electric via conversion technologies, nuclear, superconducting, nanotechnology (molecular robots), new materials.
The CEO, professional manager.	The executive team, the institutional investor, the self-employed (one's self).
A third and long stage of life.	Non-fixed, highly individualized.
Speculative real estate, information, monetary leverage.	Knowledge, delivery channels, "employees," customers, reputation
Drugs, nuclear, computerized and electronic missiles, propaganda.	Biologicals, terrorism, satellites, disabling of communications infrastructures, mind-manipulation
Einsteinian, relative, molecular, expanding universe.	Quantum, non-linear, "chaos," biological.

CHAPTER 11

Summing up

More than 43 million jobs have been eliminated since 1970. Almost three-quarters of all American households have either experienced a layoff, or know someone close who did, since 1980.

But since 1970, the American economy has created almost 70 million jobs, for a net gain of 27 million, in one of the most remarkable spurts of economic development the world has ever seen. In 1995, 45% of the jobs created in the U.S. paid more than the national average wage of $29,420. In 1992, that proportion was just 22%. One quarter of the new jobs created in 1995 paid 30% above the average, compared with only four percent of new jobs that paid that well in 1992.

What does all this mean? How will the coming **Emotile Era** play out? What threats and opportunities will people face as the transformation unfolds?

Businesses involved in *both* personal well-being and fast-moving, mobile technologies will thrive. *Information, education* and *entertainment* will underlie all other businesses.

There is great concern these days about how much is being spent on healthcare—over 15% of U.S. GDP at present. But is it necessarily bad for a people to choose to spend a lot of money on their health and wellness? We anticipate continued growth of health spending, perhaps up to 25% of U.S. GDP, with similar increases in the rest of the industrial world, when you factor in all the health-related products and services. Because that is what people will want in the **Emotile Era**. All aspects of the healthcare business, and all those careers and businesses directly and indirectly related to health, will grow.

This will include research, products, services, marketing and distribution for: Genetic engineering...mental health, including stress reduction...all forms of alternative medicine, including acupuncture, biofeedback, naturopathy, visualization, aromatherapy...preventive medicine and health management...anti-aging foods and cosmeceuticals...brain mapping...cosmetic surgery...rehabilitation...diet and nutrition...exercise...spas...memory enhancers...biosensors...sensory augmentations...sunscreens...insurance...food and water monitoring...etc., etc., etc....

Among the many other businesses and careers likely to benefit are:

Personal services: Vacation planners, personal entertainment programmers, personal editors, personal home organizers, personal beauty specialists, personal pet companions, personal wardrobe consultants, educational consultants and counselors, ergonomics advisers and equipment, and a host of other activities, in-person or electronic, that will cater to the growing need or demand for individualized and personalized services. Along with personal service goes customization. Rapidly changing technology and heated competition will once again cause dissatisfaction with the old ways of getting things done, and people will demand that their newspapers, their shoes, their financial products, their training modules and yes, even their offspring, be tailored to their personal needs and wants.

Financial security: There will be tremendous growth in services and programs for retirement planning, unemployment financing, career retraining...services aimed at the financial needs of single women, including widows and divorcees...long-term care programs for the elderly.

Personal security and safety: We can expect continued growth in monitoring and sensing services, protection services and devices, private communities, private education, encryption and espionage equipment, paramilitary services, environmental cleanup companies, water and food inspection equipment at the consumer level, home entertainment, antitheft instruments, abuse and violence centers and counseling.

Religion and spirituality: Look to continued growth in production of Scriptures (including interpretations and enactments), spiritual fiction, faith and emotional healing, guidance in ethics, schools of philosophy, cults, ethnic apparel, search for "self," human rights activism, Stewardship activities, marriages of Eastern and Western thought, survival leisure and travel, twelve-step programs and support groups.

In addition, there are almost limitless possibilities in jobs and services that focus on the changed and changing nature of relationships people will have with institutions. For example:

- Lifelong training and education in a totally revolutionized "schooling" business, with lots of alternatives, and extending from birth to death
- Outpatient services
- Part-time and contractual and temporary workers
- Network organizers
- Interactive entertainment
- Matchmakers and dating services
- Information services that bypass professional gatekeepers and go direct to the consumer
- New gatekeepers and brokers that help people navigate the ocean of information and choice
- 24-hour and 7-day/week work support.

The **Emotile Era** will present us with a blossoming of entrepreneurship. Unable to be certain of stability or permanence of employment, people will have to create their own approximations of those. That will mean creating new services that respond to the needs of people living in the new world.

Existing organizations will have to become more responsive. Recent history has demonstrated how true that is. Large, powerful organizations—IBM and Sears, to name just two—came close to disaster because of an arrogant belief that their size gave them an ability to control rather than be controlled by markets. Yes, whom the gods will destroy they first make big. So sensitivity to change and the ability to respond to it become more important.

What cannot be overlooked is the time factor. Time has speeded up. Our unit of time has gone from the year to the week, to the day, and now to the nanosecond. Responsiveness is only part of the answer...the other part is rapidity of response. Organizations, in other words, will have to become anticipatory. The Japanese auto industry's concept of "customer delight" is an example. It focuses on trying to meet customer wants even before the customer is able to articulate them.

For organizations as well as for individuals, location is becoming irrelevant. Work will continue to be disassociated from place with the enablement of technology. Intimacy will no longer necessarily be a function of proximity...networks will also be the mechanisms of closeness.

Alongside all this, we will need new concepts of how and what we measure in order to identify with any accuracy what our next economy and society are. We need, in effect, a new vocabulary. When the first motorized vehicles were called horseless carriages, we couldn't conceive of what they really were and how they would transform the world. What we call things and how we measure them are critical to understanding.

The accounting profession is now trying to come to grips with this necessity. Through its professional association, the American Institute of CPAs, it is reviewing the current models of financial reporting and auditing in order to determine how useful they will be, if at all, in whatever new world is coming. Current forms enable us to measure things that are currently measurable. The fact that they are measurable does not necessarily mean that they are useful. In the future, a business's primary assets will be its customers, its people, its knowledge and its reputation. None of these are measured on existing financial reporting forms...indeed, they are not at present measurable. It is reasonable to assume, however, that technology will eventually provide us with the means, if we have the wit, to at least come close to measuring them accurately. Economists and scientists are facing the same struggles.

The economic changes we're talking about are not confined to the U.S. A capitalist revolution is sweeping the world, creating vast new markets and demands for all kinds of goods and services. Most experts estimate that the global middle class now numbers about one and a quarter billion people. They expect that number to more than double over the next 10 years.

In the central reaches of Africa, for millenia the Gongmen controlled the means of communication by banging gongs whose rhythms only the powerful men of the tribe could interpret. Today, women are walking around in these villages with cellular phones.

The **Emotile Era** paradigm is our effort to begin the process of recognizing what lies ahead. It is, we hope, part of the new vocabulary needed to help all of us understand where we are going.